Simon Nicolas Henri Linguet

A Critical Analysis and Review, of all Mr. Voltaire's works

With Occasional Disquisitions on Epic Poetry, the Drama, Romance, &...

Simon Nicolas Henri Linguet

A Critical Analysis and Review, of all Mr. Voltaire's works
With Occasional Disquisitions on Epic Poetry, the Drama, Romance, &...

ISBN/EAN: 9783744764308

Printed in Europe, USA, Canada, Australia, Japan

Cover: Foto ©Thomas Meinert / pixelio.de

More available books at **www.hansebooks.com**

A

CRITICAL ANALYSIS

AND

REVIEW,

OF ALL

MR. VOLTAIRE's WORKS;

WITH

OCCASIONAL DISQUISITIONS

ON

EPIC POETRY,

THE

DRAMA, ROMANCE, &c.

BY MR. LINGUET.

TRANSLATED FROM THE FRENCH

BY JAMES BOARDMAN.

LONDON:

PRINTED FOR J. JOHNSON, NO. 72, ST. PAUL's
CHURCH-YARD. 1790.

GENERAL OBSERVATIONS.

———

THE republic of letters was in May, 1778, deprived of that celebrated man, whofe whole life was devoted to its fervice. Though he died at a very advanced age, his death might appear premature; for by a fate as fingular and as extraordinary as were his talents, when upwards of eighty years old, he felt none of the infirmities incident to age. His mind and his body were alike free from debility.

An indifcreet friendfhip, or interefted motives difguifed under that name, forced him into imprudencies which accelerated his death. After a period of twenty-five years, fpent in the moft peaceful retreat, in the moft regular habits of living, in as profound a calm as a conftitution fo replete with fire was capable of enjoying, he was fuddenly tranfported to the centre of diffipation. —There, his mind was thrown into an agitation no lefs violent than his perfon. The public enthufiafm, heightened by fecret anecdotes, and

B   concealed

concealed artifices, overwhelmed him with honours too weighty for his age : his health, which labor and folitude could not impair, funk under the laffitude and intoxication of a triumph renewed every day, and at every moment. By a misfortune, which it is not ufual to hear old men complain of, it was in reality excefs of pleafure that led him to the grave. Thus from beginning to the end, in every thing, and at all times, he was an extraordinary man.

It is my intention to fpeak here of his works only. Of what is merely perfonal, or relates but to his private life, I fhall fay nothing. Let us not furnifh matter to that treacherous curiofity which feeks for anecdotes of an illuftrious man, with a view rather to derive confolation under his fuperiority, than to add to his fame. The life of a fedentary writer, as Mr. Voltaire himfelf has very well obferved, is beft found in his own works. It is this part of his life only in which the liberal contemporary, or pofterity, can be truly interefted. It is from thence only that thofe who have not been perfonally acquainted with him can form a certain judgment of his character.

Mr. Voltaire appears to have poffeffed extreme fenfibility. His impetuous imagination was ftrongly affected at injuftice and vice : this natural difpofition may have fometimes rendered him

him imprudent, and even in his turn unjuſt.— During his reſidence at Cirey, the Marchioneſs du Chatelet uſed on poſt-days to ſend a meſſenger before-hand to bring the letters to the caſtle; and then ſhutting herſelf up with another friend, they opened all Mr. Voltaire's letters, ſuffering none to reach him, but thoſe in which nothing appeared capable of giving him uneaſineſs.

Perhaps we ought rather to pity, than blame, the man whoſe irritability of temper rendered this office of compaſſionate friendſhip neceſſary to his repoſe.—This organization is allied to genius; but it may hurry it into ſteps which will in time furniſh arms to hatred; to eſtimate it at the preſent day according to its juſt value, materials would be wanting, which it is now impoſſible to collect; and were it in our power to procure them, of what uſe would they be?

It muſt be confeſſed that Mr. Voltaire has run into an extreme directly oppoſite: a mercileſs ſatyriſt, when his anger was excited, he has too often deſcended even to adulation, when he thought it might prove advantageous. His flattering hyperboles have included every rank of ſociety: he has decreed titles of immortality to every claſs, from the throne to the loweſt ſpecies of literature. Whether an intereſted policy taught him

him to endeavour at difarming, by infincere panegyric, thofe dangerous defpots, whom the freedom of his other writings might have alarmed; or whether an infatiable vanity would not fuffer him to omit any means of encreafing the number of his admirers, he has left behind him but too many monuments of the facility with which he could lavifh his praifes. He wifhed not to want a fingle voice; and without fcruple, condefcended to flatter men who could not be flattered but by him alone, that he himfelf might appear an object of univerfal applaufe.

Whatever might be his character in this refpect, and perhaps in fome others, I fee no neceffity for deep inveftigation. Mr. Voltaire had faults, for he was a man; let us leave them in oblivion, with thofe of fo many millions who poffeffed ftill greater and more pernicious errors, but the memory of which is notwithftanding blotted out for ever. Let us reject thofe private and fufpicious anecdotes, which can tend only to tarnifh the honor of literature, without poffeffing even the painful merit of certainty: in the prefent impoffibility of appreciating their value, as to what concerns his principles, it were better to attribute to him virtues than vices. Let us reft fatisfied in examining his works, fince, as I have

before

before obferved,—it is from thofe only we can judge with any precifion.

What immediately ftrikes, in the immenfe collection, is their number and variety: two Epic Poems; twenty-four Tragedies; twelve Comedies, at leaft; Operas; Moral Effays, in verfe; Odes; and Epiftles on all forts of fubjects; Tales; an incredible number of little convivial pieces, fuch as of themfelves have eftablifhed the reputation of Voiture, Chapelle, and Chaulieux; Hiftories, which had alone been fufficient to occupy the life, and eftablifh the reputation of any other literary character; an Abridgement of the Theory of Sir Ifaac Newton, on Natural Philofophy and Aftronomy, too much contemned perhaps by the prejudice of thofe times, becaufe it came from a poet's pen, and ufelefs in the prefent, becaufe the fubject has been more fully inveftigated by others; but which, notwithftanding, had the merit of being the firft work in which that fubject was treated of in France [1]:

[1] This Theory, at bottom, is not more folid than that of Defcartes, but this is not the ftandard by which the work of Mr. Voltaire is to be eftimated : what has been capable of producing in men of fcience a conviction, or an enthufiafm, extending even to fanaticifm, may be fuppofed, with ftronger reafon, to have caft an illufion before a writer who was principally engaged in letters and arts.

Romances,

Romances, in which gaiety, philofophy, refined criticifm, and elegance of ftyle, fupply the place of imagination, which till then had engroffed that department of literature; Differtations without number on various points of Hiftory, the Belles Lettres, the Sciences, Philofophy, and even Jurifprudence, wherein, without the confufion, the heavinefs, and obfcurity of legal erudition, univerfal knowledge and an ardent defire of contributing to the happinefs of mankind, are conftantly difcoverable; this paffion unhappily extended to indifcretion on a delicate fubject, on which filence is better than difcuffion; a Commentary, full of tafte and impartiality, on the firft and moft prolific of Tragic Poets: and finally, an Epiftolary Correfpondence, more extenfive, perhaps, than any man, of any nation, or of any country, has been found capable of maintaining; a correfpondence of which, if we may form an opinion from what has already tranfpired of it, ever ingenious, ever agreeable, and almoft always on his part inftructive :—this may ferve to give fome idea of the literary labors of Mr. Voltaire.

When we reflect moreover that he travelled a great deal in his youth: that he fpent thirty years in the diffipation of courts, and in the moft brilliant circles; that he underftood Italian,

I   Spanifh,

Spanish, and English; that he had read, as it appears, attentively, in the originals the best authors in each of these languages; and that in the midst of these interruptions and occupations he was by no means indifferent to his own affairs, which were arranged and kept in an order and exactness equal to his personal vigilance and regularity; that he inspected his bills, and balanced his accounts, with as much punctuality as a man who had no other business; our astonishment at such a prodigious fertility of talents must without doubt be increased. But I ought here to make two observations, which will partly serve to explain this enigma.

First, the youth of almost all our celebrated authors has been usually spent either in painful struggles, or in those embarrassments which attend on what is called the choice of a profession; they are tyrannized over for a long time, or at least impeded in their progress by the importunities of their relations, if not by their own necessities: there is hardly one in whom the first efforts of genius have not been combated as a passion which it was necessary to repress, or at least to watch over as something dangerous. Enfeebled by distress, still more grievous than restraint, it was even amidst the toil of ignoble occupations, very opposite to the natural bent of

their

their inclination, that the greater part have given birth to thofe productions which have eftablifhed their fame.

There are therefore very few amongft them of whofe abilities the public may be fuppofed capable of forming an adequate opinion.—At an age when cultivation, exercife, and liberty, are neceffary to nourifh, call forth, and ftrengthen their talents ; care withers, and flavery ftifles them. When the reputation is eftablifhed, it is then again too late, they then become enervated by reft and plenty. When young, literary men are removed from the world, with which a moderate commerce, fought for on the one hand without degradation, and granted on the other without the pomp of patronage, might ferve greatly to their improvement ; at a more advanced period of life, they are hurried into it, courted, careffed, and become fo abforbed in its pleafures, as to have no time left for labor and ftudy.

It was far different with Mr. Voltaire. Every thing feemed to concur in favoring and affifting that love of glory and of fcience which he inherited from nature. A fettled fortune which devolved to him at an early period of life, left him in his youth at full liberty to gratify this paffion, and freed him from thofe obftructions which

which a timid family would not have failed to throw in his way.

The care of his youth was entrufted to the Jefuits, whofe knowledge of the human mind, and whofe care to excite emulation in their pupils, at leaft cannot be denied them.   At thirteen years old, they announced him as a prodigy, who would produce a revolution in literature.   Thus, even at this early age, had he acquired, through their favor, a fpecies of celebrity.

Ninon de l'Enclos, that celebrated beauty who arrived at fame by a road through which other women are conducted to infamy, fhe who, after having been adored by the old men of the laft century, was idolized by the young ones of the prefent; who was regarded as one of the arbiters of good tafte of every kind, made honorable mention of him; fhe diftin-guifhed him in her will, and, by the nature of her legacy, which was a fum of money to pur-chafe books, pays him a tribute due, in her opinion, to his rifing genius.

The friends of Ninon introduced him to the Vendomes, the Chaulieux, and to the Duchefs of Maine and her courtiers; philofophic voluptu-aries, perhaps fomewhat fatyrical, but with en-lightened minds, and who retained all the elegance and urbanity of the age of Lewis the XIVth.

united

united with that liberality of fentiment which prevailed at his death. Amongft fuch characters, there was much to be learnt by a young man, more efpecially in whatever related to tafte.

Thus ufhered into life, his firft productions arrefted the attention of all France; his youth gained him the favour of the women and the court; even thus early, the encouragement he received was general, the criticifm and malignity of the few was loft in the admiration and applaufe of the many. If his firft fuccefíes drew on him fome rancorous foes in the lower departments of literature, they amply repaid him in the protection of feveral perfons of high rank, who became the more warmly attached to him, as from his fortune, he was placed above all interefted views; and as he feemed to folicit his friends only to co-operate with him in promoting his reputation, they had it in their power to afford him proofs of their attachment on very eafy terms.

To complete his good fortune, when he commenced his literary career he found no rivals who could, or ought to have indulged a hope of eclipfing him. Rouffeau was overwhelmed with misfortunes. Crebillon and La Motte did not feem to threaten a very formidable conteft: little penetration and felf-love feems to have been neceffary in the author of Oedipus to perceive that

not

not only the theatre, but even the poetry of France, would shortly have him alone for their support.

Add to all these favourable circumstances, those gifts he had received from nature; a prodigious memory, a quick conception, a state of health sufficiently robust to sustain the most arduous labor, and too delicate to bear any other excess; a facility of composition, which lessening the fatigue of study, rendered relaxation less necessary to him, and his triumphs more numerous and frequent.—It may by this time be conceived, that, with less natural abilities than Mr. Voltaire possessed, he must have excelled all his contemporaries.

Lastly, let it be recollected, that having been early initiated in the most brilliant circles, in such as were most capable of forming his taste, and polishing his stile; two thirds of his life, that is to say, those years which other writers lose, as I have before observed, in struggling with the difficulties of life, those which are lost between the desire of establishing a name, and the necessity of obtaining a provision; that time which others almost wholly devote to enjoy in ease, the honors they have earned with difficulty, was by him dedicated to retreat and to sedulous application. Let it be remembered too,

too, that having from his youth conſtantly had at his command books, ſecretaries, and copyiſts, and conſequently been placed in a ſituation where no opportunity of gaining, or retaining his ideas, could be wanting, he had it in his power to ſpare much time, which being however employed, in ſome meaſure doubled his literary capacity and reſources. Arriving at his laborious retreat, with immenſe materials as we may ſay both in his head and in his port folio, the ſurpriſe will partly ceaſe, that he was able to multiply, with a fertility of invention which hitherto ſeemed peculiar to writers on divinity, or of romance, thoſe ſtriking productions, many of which are worthy of being regarded as models of our literature.

But this is not all. Perhaps we are too apt to annex the idea of extraordinary to the union of ſeveral talents in the ſame man; perhaps it is only thought ſo uncommon, becauſe prejudice has taught us to conſider it as impoſſible. We deride thoſe Egyptian legiſlators who confined their ſubjects to the cultivation not only of a ſingle art, but even to part of one: this appears to us abſurd, and we notwithſtanding imitate them in the arts of the mind.

Should a phyſician, or even a lawyer, diſcover a taſte for letters, it is ſufficient to diſcredit

credit him in his profeſſion, render him ſuſ-
pected among his fellows, and of little eſtima-
tion with the public. If a poet chances to
write on ſome ſerious ſubject in proſe, a hiſtory
for example, or a treatiſe on geometry, or le-
giſlation, every one is ſtruck with aſtoniſhment;
the ſucceſs even of theſe extravagancies makes
no addition to his former reputation, and may
do it an injury: ſhould a ſoldier hazard a few
rhymes, whether on his own accompliſhments,
his reputation, or his gallantry, he may gain
ſome applauſe, but reſt aſſured, he will not, on
that account, be more eſteemed in his corps:
his military talents will moſt aſſuredly be leſs
regarded; and he may think himſelf happy if a
ſecret murmur does not prevail, that with his
poetical trifling, he is likely to do little honor to
the regiment.

It may neverthelefs afford much more rational
ground for ſurprize, to find a man whoſe capacity
is confined to a ſingle point, than to meet with
others in whom ſeveral are found united. —Parts,
in general, have a near affinity to each other;
and perhaps, there are very few, if any, that are
abſolutely incompatible.

What is it we mean by genius? It is the facility of conceiving, and the aptitude of expreſſing
ideas whether by words or actions; and ſhall
theſe

thefe powers have but one application? Shall
they be abforbed in the firft employment, which
chance or reflection may have pointed out? It
were to fay that the pencil with which Titian
painted his Venus's, would not ferve alike to
form the Titans of a Julio Romano.

It might feem, indeed, that thofe turbulent
qualities which conftitute a hero, would be rarely
found united with that ferenity of mind neceffary
in a good orator, or an able writer; experience,
however, has fhewn that they are by no means
incompatible.   Thucydides, Xenophon, Cæfar,
even Cicero, and feveral others united them;
and if in modern times fuch inftances are rarely
to be met with, it is owing to the prejudice I
have mentioned.   It is this which has feparated and divided the different departments
of fcience, beyond all refource, and has thrown
up fuch barriers between them as nature never
intended.

Thofe at leaft who are embarked in the tranquil
departments of fcience, have not at prefent
even the leaft incompatibility to contend a-
gainft: yet when a poet touches on natural
philofophy, aftronomy, &c. we decry the attempt as rafh and indifcreet: in our colleges,
however, are we not told that the knowledge of
Homer was univerfal, and defcended even to a

particular

particular acquaintance with the lowest mecha-
nifm ? Was not Plato, whofe profe is much
more poetical than the verfe of many poets, a
geometrician ? Has he not too much indulged
in the theory of that fcience, in digefting his
philofophical ideas ? Has not Ariftotle alfo written
on natural hiftory, politics, logic, poetry, and
morality ? And was not Cicero equally eminent as a moralift, and a profound differtator
on thofe points of philofophy moft interefting to
mankind ?

If more examples are wanting, has there been
one eminent painter, at leaft of thofe who have
given a free fcope to their genius, who has confined himfelf to that art alone ? Michael Angelo
was a great painter, a ftill more eminent fculptor,
and an equally good architect. Leonardo de
Vinci produced excellent pictures, while engaged -
in the ftudy of mufic, in drawing plans of canals,·
and in works wherein he difplayed all the boldnefs and capacity of an excellent engineer.
Raphael was likewife both a poet and a mufician.
In fhort, if inftances of this verfatility of genius
are rare in modern times, we muft attribute it,
firft, to the effects of that prejudice which, in
exalting it into a kind of prodigy, takes from
thofe whofe natural abilities might enable them
to renew the illuftrious examples, the idea even

of

of making the attempt.—Secondly, to thofe impediments and depreffing cares which, as I have before remarked, almoft ever attend the juvenile years of men of parts, and which deprive them at once both of power and inclination to embrace the various departments of fcience: though its branches are nearly allied, and interwoven with each other; though the fame genius which animated a Virgil or a Racine, would have made a Raphael; though an Hippocrates might have fhone out a Tacitus, had he begun early to delineate hiftorical characters, inftead of collecting medical aphorifms; and though the only difference between them confifted, perhaps, in habits contracted at an early age: habits by which they were fettered during the remainder of their lives, and they died not only without difcovering, but even without fufpecting in themfelves the talents they poffeffed.

Mr. Voltaire, even at his firft outfet, being freed from thefe fhackles, poffeffed his abilities in their full force, and as thefe were great from the prodigality of nature, fo were they enlarged by inceffant application. He had already attained the art of increafing his varied productions with eafe, often fuccefsfully contending with thofe writers who had been exclufively engaged in their refpective departments.

This

This confideration detracts nothing from his merit, and may ferve to leffen the concern of the public under its lofs by the emulation it has a tendency to excite in others.—It was even necef-fary to enlarge upon it here, in order to refcue his memory from the reproach but too often repeated during his life, of levity or indifcretion, founded on the variety of his productions.

In reviewing his works we fhall divide them according to their different fubjects, and fuc-ceffively proceed to examine the refpective me-rits of each clafs: he was a poet and of every kind: he was a profe writer and diftinguifhed himfelf on all fubjects; he has treated on phi-lofophy and the demonftrative fciences; but above all, it was to morality and that part of reafoning which comprehends politics, and more efpecially religion, that he particularly devoted himfelf.—Hence naturally refults the order of this inquiry.

C   FIRST

FIRST PART

OF

MR. VOLTAIRE's

POETICAL WORKS.

EPIC POEMS.

MR. Voltaire made two efforts to gain the
Epic Laurel, denied to every French writer before him who had the ambition to afpire
to it. Has he been more fuccefsful than his
predeceffors? Has he vindicated the French
nation from the fuppofed difgrace of not having
as yet produced an epic poem? Of remaining
wholly deftitute of that glory granted with fo
much honor to Greece, and lavifhed, as it were,
on Italy?

Many are of opinion that he has not. Some
there are too, who willing to reconcile their
feverity with a patriotic fentiment, and con-

ceiving

ceiving the national honor interefted in its being
able to boaft on any terms of one epic poem at
leaft, have dignified Telemachus with that epithet; as if a romance in profe, could properly
be reckoned among the treafures of French
poetry ; or as though the univerfal reproach under which our language has labored of pretended
fterility in the epopeia were not in reality a dif-
paragement to it.

But the truth is, that we not only have col-
lections of verfes of this defcription, but our
language has proved as prolific in this fpecies
of compofition as all the other languages in
Europe put together. An epic poem fignifies a
recital made by the poet, in contradiftinction to
the drama, wherein a fet of perfonages are introduced, by whofe fpeaking and acting the
piece is conducted. Now it appears to me very
abfurd that it fhould be faid of a language that
it is incapable of producing fuch works, while it
poffeffes in the proportion of more than ten to one
of them; as we might inftance in the Louifiad
of P. Lemoine, the Alaric of Scudery, the Clovis
of Defmaretes, the Pucelle of Chapelain, &c. &c.

But it will be faid of thefe recitals, of thefe
epic poems, are they good ? This is quite another
matter. If in every department of literature
the name that diftinguifhes each fpecies were to
be

be applied to fuch works only as had attained the height of perfection, would the titles of tragedies, comedies, odes, &c. be fo confidently applied as at prefent? The Italians do not refufe the title of epic poets either to Triffino or Dante, who are not heard of beyond the Alps, and who are in trifling repute with their own countrymen. The Englifh unanimoufly decree that honor to Milton, who remained a long time in obfcurity and contempt even among themfelves, and who is not yet in general eftimation with other nations. Why fhould we be more fcrupulous or unjuft towards thofe, who amongft us have moved in the fame fphere?

It is true that the delicacy of the language and the refined tafte of the nation have not been fufficiently attended to by our heroic poets. With a minute attention to every other rule, they have failed in that grand particular, which fhould be univerfally deemed of moft importance in every literary production, that of pleafing and creating an intereft by the general defign of the work, the epifodes, and the ftile: they have poffeffed imagination without tafte; and compofed verfes without poetry: it is this, that hath condemned their works: and although they are at leaft as much entitled to the epithet of epic poems as the Iliad itfelf, they are properly excluded from the number of thofe productions

deftined

deſtined to immortality. May that portion of Mr. Voltaire's works which, agreeably to the definition I have laid down, are inconteſtably epic, expect a happier fate? Let us enquire; to begin with the Henriade.

I ſhall not examine if Mr. Voltaire has exactly obſerved the rules of Ariſtotle, or of Father le Boſſu, or whether in any work, either poetical or profaic, any other can be prefcribed than the univerſal ones of pleaſing, affecting, and inſtructing. Rules can have no other end than that of rendering a work capable of producing thefe effects; whoever has ſucceeded in this reſpect, has obſerved all the rules, or fuch as he has tranſgreſſed were not neceſſary.

Among the ſmall number of productions on which, by common ſuffrage, this merit is conferred, may be diſtinguiſhed the Iliad, the Æneid, the Jeruſalem Delivered, and the Orlando Furioſo. Now I can difcern no real refemblance in thefe pieces, but in the excellence they poſſeſs in common, of exciting attention, and intereſt, of occupying the imagination, and rouſing the affections, of prefenting to the mind a variety of events, either ſtriking from their grandeur, affecting from their tenderneſs or ſimplicity, interwoven with art, and rendered pleaſing by the charms of poetry. To eſtimate the excellence

lence of the Henriade we have therefore only to enquire, if it poffeffes any of thefe charaƈteriftics.

It muſt be inſtantly apparent, that the fubjeƈt is in itſelf the moſt happy, the moſt fertile, and moſt truly epic, that any poet has hitherto made choice of; that it is admirably calculated for the developement of the nobleſt paſſions, and of courſe very proper for ſupplying ingenious epiſodes, and intereſting narrations.

The Iliad turns upon a domeſtic and perſonal quarrel between two princes. The argument of the Æneid is a relation of the travels and voyages of a ſingle fugitive, in ſearch of an aſylum for himſelf and ſome of his diſtreſſed countrymen who ſurround him. The Jeruſalem preſents at firſt view a grander fubjeƈt, that of recovering the Holy Land : but, in faƈt, the true objeƈt of the poem, is the ſiege of a ſingle city, and that part of the enterprize which is moſt reſpeƈtable, is not that which the poet has endeavoured to render moſt conſpicuous. With regard to Arioſto, he appears to have no objeƈt at all; at leaſt his only one ſeems to be, to unite in his Orlando all the qualities in which the excellence of ſuch a poem conſiſts.

Thus of the four works I have enumerated, whatever beauty, grandeur, and machinery they contain, is wholly to be attributed to the imagi-

C 4   nation

nation of the poet. Like Prometheus, they at once gave exiftence and animation to their Pandoras.

In the Henriade, on the other hand, hiftory fupplied a ground of action, characters, and incidents in great variety, ready at hand. We fee a great kingdom divided into two parties, who wage the moft cruel war againft each other. Religion becomes intermixed with ambition, and increafes their animofity. A foreign family, by availing itfelf of their mutual diffenfion, forms the daring project of overturning and ufurping the throne. Thefe defigns are oppofed by a hero endowed with every great and amiable virtue, who, fupported by his perfonal merit alone, and the effect of an invincible firmnefs and dignity of mind, at length fucceeds in extinguifhing the flames of civil war.

Thus, whatever intrigues and violence boundlefs ambition may create among the nobles; all the tranfports, fervility, and crimes, with which fanaticifm and habits of obedience may infpire the populace; all that attachment to royalty, and thofe generous virtues which true heroifm gives birth to in that clafs of men, more efpecially devoted to the paths of honor; all naturally enter into the reprefentation.

The

The state of men's minds, at the time of which we are speaking, was no less interesting, nor less favorable to epic poetry, than the circumstances themselves: on every side new objects croud on the beholder: the policy of states altering with the situation of the world, which within fifty years was enlarged, if we may so say, by one-half, till then unknown. Commerce, by a revolution no less surprising, had from the centre of Europe connected the extremities of Asia. Philip too, whom these wonderful discoveries seemed principally intended to aggrandize, was the great enemy to the hero of the Henriade, and by a singular fatality, while assisting the revolted subjects of the latter in expelling their lawful sovereign, was himself braved and conquered by his own subjects, whom the oppression of his government had excited to revolt. That monarch, while supporting the League, was unable to reduce the United Provinces to obedience, confederated together for their mutual defence against his tyranny.

As to characters, history at this period furnishes a number of remarkable ones already delineated, and as it should seem formed to make a striking figure in an Epic Poem. Among foreign nations we discover a Philip II, gloomy, dissembling, bloody, and hypocritical; an Elizabeth,

beth, crafty, interefted, jealous of her glory, and ftill more of her tranquility; a Sixtus V. haughty and impetuous, but enlightened and juft, more of a king than a pontiff; a prince of Orange, ambitious of power and glory, but wife enough to perceive that Holland once feparated from Spain, could exift by liberty alone; laboring himfelf therefore to deliver her from the bondage, without wifhing to fupply the place of the tyrant whom he was to dethrone, and contenting himfelf with a reward founded on gratitude; a duke of Parma, a great general, phlegmatic, ftill more ambitious perhaps than the prince of Orange, but reftrained by oppofite duties, and lefs affifted by favorable events.

In France we fee a Henry III. weak and imprudent, enervated by pleafure, and degraded by trifling; intermingling devotion and diforder, fcandal and religion; a duke d'Epernon rendered odious by his pride and his caprice, ufing his fortune with an infolence equal to the bafenefs by which it was acquired. The two Birons men of courage and of parts, but the one more defirous of riches and of power, than of the public welfare; the other vain and prefumptuous, and calculated to lofe in extravagant projects the merit and reward of his brilliant actions; a Sully haughty and œconomical, and
animated

animated with almoft an equal attachment towards his religion, his country, and his fovereign; a Crillon the intrepid emulator of Bayard,
The fecond knight without fear and without reproach,
equally daring at court, and in the field of action; a Briffac, and d'Aumont, illuftrious from
their own and their anceftors exploits; a duchefs of Montpenfier at firft diftinguifhed by
her beauty, afterwards by her intrigues; enraged
by refentment, and feeking by the exile, depo-
fition, and even the death of Henry the Third,
to revenge a perfonal affront rather than to ferve
her party, or punifh the deftroyer of her family; a duke of Mayenne cool, ambitious,
poffeffed of great abilities, but without the fury
of an enthufiaft, or the vices which perhaps are
neceffary for the leader of a party; and a thoufand others might be pointed out in the church,
the army, the law, and among the commonalty.

Henry IV. is here certainly furrounded by a
greater number of principal charaéters than are
to be found in the whole Æneid, and as many
as the Iliad itfelf prefents. We fee them ready
pourtrayed, and it is before the eyes of their grand-
children that the poet brings them again into
exiftence; an advantage that Homer alone poffeffed among the epic poets, for it may be con-
jeétured

jectured that he, like Mr. Voltaire, wrote in an age not far removed from that of his heroes [2].

The latter then, both from the subject and the events, had a thousand times less difficulties to encounter, and more resources to resort to, than any of his predecessors. All he had to do, was by a happy fiction, to reanimate these dormant particles scattered abroad over the wide field of history, to set them in motion on a theatre properly disposed to exhibit them to advantage, and to form them into a body, which

[2] It is an advantage in point of interest, perhaps a disadvantage in point of poetry, in the liberty of inventing fictions; and in the arrangement of facts. But Homer was not embarrassed with these difficulties: he has availed himself of every bold and grand idea his imagination dictated to him; which he was not deterred from adopting by the fear of offending or contradicting history. Speaking to the children, he has drawn their fathers so great, that the mind of man has never yet been capable of producing any thing which could do away their impression.

With an equal portion of genius it is possible then at any time to have produced the like prodigy. A divine spirit of poetry is necessary to metamorphose into demi-gods men so near ourselves; but possessed of the genius, any one may perform the miracle. That the characters should be recent and their memory dear to us, must then be attended with superior advantage. What Frenchman would not more readily admit the apotheosis of Henry the Great than that of Childebrand.

having

having truth for its animating principle, fhould be clothed and adorned with all the foft illufions of fable, and the richeft embellifhments of poetry. This is what the Henriade ought to have been. Let us now fee what it is. It is impoffible to conceal the avowal: no; the Henriade has nothing of all this. It is wholly deficient in action; the author has not even availed himfelf of the numberlefs valuable materials which were at his difpofal: he has not added to the fubject any of thofe ornaments which the nature of it required, and with which an imagination tolerably fertile might fo eafily have enriched it; he has even weakened the few embellifhments which he has endeavoured to borrow from preceding poets.—This I fhall endeavour to explain.

Of the inaction, and confequently the coldnefs which prevails throughout this poem, we need but open it to be fenfible. It will be found to abound with beautiful defcriptions, but hardly a fingle animated being. They are highly finifhed medallions, adapted to the decoration of a gallery, not living characters crouding into it.

To begin with Sixtus the Fifth. It is in his reign that the poet fends Difcord to the Vatican in fearch of Policy, to come and corrupt the

Sor-

Sorbonne: this certainly was the occasion wherein he should act in the poem, at least as much as he really does in history; in any case, it is from him that Policy ought to receive her orders and instructions. But there is nothing of all this.— We find, contained in fifty verses, a very fine description of ancient and modern Rome, of the different revolutions of the Holy See, of its losses and acquisitions; but, after all, it is but a description. A portrait of Sixtus the Fifth follows in eight verses, after which he disappears and is never again heard of. It is not from any regard to his dignity that the author has thus consigned him to oblivion, since the principal quality by which he is here distinguished, is that of fraud; for of eight verses which relate to this pontiff, seven are taken up in describing his propensity to cheating, which has not even the merit of being an historical fact.

It is the same with the queen of England, and the king of Spain, Henry the Third, and the principal French officers. These the poet should more especially have endeavoured to engage in action, to have placed them in situations wherein their virtues or defects might have been rendered conspicuous, in order to contribute to

the

the interest and general design of the poem; and this is what he has not done; the greater part of those characters which I have before enumerated are not even mentioned, or he has been satisfied with barely mentioning them.

Henry the Third is introduced in a narrative at London but to be censured [3], and at Paris but to be assassinated. Biron represented as the bosom friend of Henry the Fourth, as the Hephestion of this Alexander, appears but once, solely for the purpose of receiving this eulogium, after which we know not what becomes of him. Mornay is brought on three or four times, twice to furnish an occasion for saying the same thing in different terms, namely, that he is a philosophic leader detesting war, notwithstanding en-

---

[3] We may even say to be cruelly and indecently traduced. —It is his ally, his presumptive heir, his ambassador, who speaks, and while uniting in his own person these three several characters, he twice charges him in direct terms in the same verse with baseness. Speaking of the duke of Guise, his crimes and his death, Henry the Fourth says,

The king from whom he wrested his authority,
Basely endur'd, and meanly reveng'd his wrongs.

This is true, but was it the part of his representative to declare it. In every page of the Henriade may be traced the philosopher in the author, or the author philosophizing; the personages themselves never speak in their own character.

gaged

gaged in it from complaifance to others, but without deftroying any one.

> " Detefting war, and fingularly brave,
> " Knew boldly to face death, but never gave."

which, though very fine in philofophy, is very dry and infipid in a poem, more efpecially as this fage in his whole conduct confines himfelf to his part of an automaton, and acts elfewhere with as little energy as he does in battle.

Thofe perfonages who are fometimes placed in fituations fomewhat animated, retain them but for a fhort time: it is even by forced epithets, or adventitious helps, that they are inefficiently characterifed. We have the valiant Turenne, and the prudent Mayenne, Harley that noble leader, and Potier the man of virtue, together with the Sixteen, rendered eminent among the factious by their crimes.

But Turenne is a valiant knight, who fights a duel, and who is heard of neither before nor afterwards. After Harley has been put into the Baftile by Buffy le Clerc, the account of which occupies about thirty lines of the poem, after Potier has made a fpeech to the ftates, which contains with all its appendages about fixty, they both difappear never to be feen more: the ftates them-

felves

felves are but the apparition of a moment, and have no influence on any thing.

The duke of Mayenne, the fecond character, and in a degree the hero of the poem, the Hector of the French, who at leaft for a time fhould divide our intereft and regard; the duke of Mayenne is himfelf but a fpectator. In battle it is his brother, and not he, who diftinguifhes himfelf. In the fanatical proceffion of the monks, he looks on without interfering. In the preparation for the regicide of Jacques Clement,

> ————" he fees the fatal blow,
> " And more he knows, than what he feems to know."

He appears to the ftates

> " With all the ornaments of kingly pride,"

but to be told he is but a fubject; and he hears it without a word in reply: he fpeaks as little as he acts.

Thofe fixteen daring commoners, the principal fources of the rebellion, thofe heads of the League, thofe rivals of the duke of Mayenne, placed at his fide, and, as the poet fays,

> " Ennobled by their enmity to kings,
> " And feated by the people next the throne;"

D   thefe

thefe formidable fixteen, ferve in the Henriade
but to commit the parliament to the Baftile,
and afterwards fhut themfelves up in a cavern
with a Jewifh forcerer, to accomplifh the deftruction of the two kings, by thrufting needles
into waxen images.   Laftly, Henry the Fourth,
towards whom every thing ought to tend as to
a common centre, and from whom all fhould
be infpired with exiftence and motion; Henry
the Fourth himfelf is fcarcely more animated
than the reft.   Of the ten little cantos which
compofe the poem, one is occupied in relating
his voyage to England, two in a very fine ftory,
but productive of nothing, and which gives not
birth to any event whatfoever; a fourth in a
journey to heaven, performed in a dream, which
likewife is nugatory in its confequences; and a
fifth he fpends in the arms of a little girl whom
he meets by accident, for whom he forgets all
his ferious concerns, and whom he abandons as
liftlefsly as he firft took her.

In the five remaining ones what does he do?
With regard to the eighth and tenth, wherein
may be traced fome of the features of the times,
we do not even find in the Henriade the Henry
of hiftory.   We may with fafety affirm, that as
in the epifode of Anet his frailties poffefs a

5   ftronger

stronger relief than his virtues, at least they are described at greater length.

How much unlike the other poets I have mentioned! What fire and animation is there in the Iliad during the abfence of Achilles? How many leaders on both fides are covered with glory, without its being possible for us to forget that the hero is not present. It is true, when he does appear, he shines alone; but with what art has Homer preserved the honor of Diomede, Agamemnon, and Ulysses? He has caused them all to be wounded in some of the preceding battles, fo that it at least remains a doubt whether it is by the presence of Achilles or their own forced inaction, that they are thrown into a kind of eclipse.

There is lefs action in the Eneid; and this, indeed, is the principal objection made to that admirable poem: but, notwithstanding this, its calm is a whirlwind when compared to the dead ftilnefs of the Henriade. Let a comparifon be drawn between the tender Dido, and the philofophic Elizabeth, or the eafy Gabrielle; the games of Aceftes at Anchifes's tomb, or the vifit to the venerable Evander, &c. with the short morning repaft in the ifland of Jerfey, or the dry prophecy of the gentleman hermit; the Sybil and her hell, with the dream infpired by

St. Louis with its detail; in short, the negoci-
ations, descriptions, and battles, with which the
last six books of the Latin poem abound, together with that continual attention of the author, to place before the Romans not only their
history, but what was still more intersting, the
fables of their anceftors; let this be compared
with the void of the Henriade, its silence on all
these subjects, and if any then presume to censure the indolence of the pious Æneas amidst
so many animated objects, what will be said to
that of the Bourbon of the sixteenth century,
imitated and rivalled by every object around
him.

In the Jerusalem Delivered, witchcraft, perhaps, holds too considerable a part; but the remainder is full of life and fire. We sympathize
with Armida when she bears away Rinaldo; we
partake of her despair when he quits her; we
lament with Herminia; and deplore with Tancred the loss of his Clorinda, though it is his
indifference which causes the tears of the princess
of Antioch to flow. The battles of Tasso, as
well described as those of Homer, are more varied, and he had the art of introducing into
them Armida, Armida ever amiable, ever interesting, because she is always animated.

Ariosto

Ariofto himfelf, whofe ftile of compofition is half ferious and half burlefeque, who feems to give up the reins to an imagination wild, and without any fixed object; even Ariofto himfelf has not one of his characters, and their number is incredible, who is not in action; not one whofe fuccefs does not afford us pleafure, or in whofe misfortunes we do not fympathize.

In fhort, each of thefe poems is a mine of characters, all widely differing, and placed in fituations each more interefting than the other. They afford an inexhauftible fund of fubject-matter for tragedies, operas, and romances, and the fubjects are fuch as are worthy the imagination of their feveral authors.——Can a fingle one of this nature be found in the Henriade? Whence is it that fictions thus founded in abfurdity, fhould, under the hand of other poets, have produced fuch admirable compofitions, while a ground-work fo true, fo noble, fo fertile, and fo grand, fhould under that of Mr. Voltaire, have given birth to nothing but puppets without motion and without expreffion? The coloring, as I before faid, is pleafing, but it is a reprefentation of dead, not living characters.

There is befides in epic poetry another kind of action, perhaps no lefs neceffary to it, which though not arifing immediately from the ground-

D 3   work

work of the piece, nor having any direct relation to its intereſt, does not fail to increaſe it,
and which leaves the reader in a ſoft repoſe, without cauſing him to forget the heroes : this is
either in the occaſional deſcription of countries
through which the characters are made to travel,
of cuſtoms either foreign or domeſtic depicted
in the epiſodes, or of ſuch arts and ſciences as
are moſt capable of exciting curioſity and producing lively imagery.

It is here that the poet may, and even ought,
to diſplay all his knowledge. As he ſpeaks in
the firſt perſon, as he claims to be inſpired by
the muſes, he is at full liberty to create incidents, and as it ſhould be his firſt care to be
always affecting, inſtructive, or entertaining, he
may here without ſcruple diſcover the full extent
of his acquirements, provided that his inſtruc-
tions are ſeaſonable, and his learning free from
pedantry.

This is what Homer and Virgil did not
fail to do. The Iliad and the Odyſſey are
ſketches of natural philoſophy, policy, hiſtory,
arts and ſcience, and geography ; at leaſt in the
latter as far as the knowledge of the Greeks extended, that is to ſay, to a part of the ſhores
and iſlands of the Mediterranean, for to theſe
limits were confined their knowledge of the earth.

The

The manners, cuſtoms, religion, arts, and laws, the boundaries of ſtates, and the intereſts both public and private, of communities and individuals, are all here pourtrayed : and this ſecret charm which immediately excited the attachment of the cotemporary, has probably contributed at leaſt as much as the merit of the poetry itſelf, to eſtabliſh that reputation of Homer which time ſeems incapable of imparing.

Virgil has been careful to imitate Homer in theſe reſpects.—The boundaries of the world ſince the ſiege of Troy were conſiderably enlarged, and the field of the Æneid is accordingly extended in proportion.

He firſt preſents his hero in Africa; but a narrative ably conducted brings the reader back to Aſia, and makes him a ſpectator of the deſtruction of Troy, the moſt celebrated city of that part of the globe.

This leads to the amours of Dido, whom if Eneas had forſaken with more honor, the piece might have vied with every other as the *chef d'œuvre* of epic poetry; and, perhaps, in ſpite of this defect, may ſtill be regarded as ſuch.— Arrived in Italy, Eneas begins by making his deſcent into the infernal regions, which gives occaſion to the fineſt repreſentation of the religion, myſteries, and philoſophy, and to a diſ-

play

play of every grand and ingenious idea on thefe
fubjects, which the intercourfe with the Greeks
had transferred to the modern Romans. But
while thus engaged in a foreign fyftem of philofophy, the poet does not omit to defcribe by
their ancient names the inhabitants of Italy, their
original codes of legiflation and their mythology, and even the old topography of Rome
and its environs: in fhort, he has collected together all that antiquity can offer to the memory
as facred and valuable.

Neither Taffo nor Ariofto poffeffes this excellence in an equal degree, but they are by no
means wholly deftitute of it. The manners of
the times are at leaft reprefented, the cuftoms
of chivalry are obferved; we travel with their
heroes; the whole world paffes in review before the
reader; and though their games, particularly in
Ariofto, are altogether as extraordinary as their
perfonages, we are lefs fhocked at their prodigies and eccentricities, than we are amufed by
their machinery and continual buftle. It prevents monotony, and we admire the art by
which the poet, always mafter of his fubject,
fteers without error through the immenfe laby-
rinth, from which he feems to have taken no
previous meafures of extricating himfelf.

In

In the Henriade, the author has prescribed to himself a narrow circle, out of which he departs no more than his hero. The latter is conducted into England, for no other end than to meet St. Bartholomew there. This voyage gives occasion to forty very fine verses on the government and character of the English, but not one circumstance which brings them into action, or incorporates them into the poem; not one event relative to that island, which even in those days was capable of affording so many beautiful episodes.

Discord is transported to Rome, and this furnishes matter, as I have before observed, for a description of sixty verses, but a description wholly speculative and antithetical, without one action or a single fact; when Discord disappears, Rome disappears likewise from the poet and the reader.

With regard to Spain and its inhabitants, all that we find of them in the Henriade is the epithet of old Castilian applied to Philip the IId. which is neither very pleasing nor instructive.

After the conversation at London, and the journey to Rome, the most distant country which appears in our poem is Normandy. The whole scene lies in the vicinity of Paris: the reader is perpetually chained to this spot as well as the
poet:

poet: not a single digreffion to divert him from
it; not an idea to relieve him from the painful
and difgraceful fpectacle, of the French enflaved
by tyrannical ufurpers, and in rebellion againft a
monarch as virtuous as he was legal; not an allu-
fion to the manners of the times, or to the ancient
cuftoms, or if there are any fuch, they are falfe.

Such is the opening of the Sixth Canto.

> " In France an ancient cuftom we retain,
> When death, refiftlefs, ends the monarch reign;
> When deftiny cuts fhort the fmooth defcent,
> And all the royal pedigree is fpent;
> The people to their former rights reftor'd,
> May change the laws, or chufe their future lord.
> The ftates in council reprefent the whole,
> Elect the king, and limit his controul:
> Thus our renown'd forefathers did ordain,
> That Capet fhould fucceed to Charlemagne.
> The League, with vain prefumption, arrogates
> This right, and haftens to convene the ftates."

Nothing can be lefs correct in every fenfe
than thefe affertions. Can that be called cuftom,
which is never done? For it never has happened
in France, that the people have difpofed of the
crown, from the blood royal becoming extinct.
In the two changes which our hiftory prefents,
the depofed race had ftill fome branches remaining. Childeric the IIId. was dethroned by Pepin,
but he furvived his degradation, and his youth

gave

gave reason to expect he might have an offspring. The descendants of Pepin experienced nearly the same treatment at the hands of Hugh Capet: but it was not the parliament, or the states, who conferred the crown on the latter, he possessed himself of it by force, and at the time when the posterity of Charlemagne was not extinct. The throne was disputed by a great uncle of the late king, who was not the only surviving Prince of the blood.

It was not the genealogy of Henry the IVth. which was contested in the assembly of the states at Paris: the legitimacy of his right, founded on his filial claim, was never questioned: the League felt this, and so well did they agree as to the right of his house to the throne, that they acknowledged the Cardinal de Bombon, his uncle, as king. It was to his religion they objected: it was as a heretic, and as no otherwise incompetent to the succession, that they assumed a right to exclude him from it.

Such deviations from historical truth are the more inexcusable, as no sort of beauty results from them.

These states too furnish matter for a beautiful episode: this was the proper place to have spoken of their ancient rights and customs; and to have brought forward into action the members most
interested

interested in the impending decifion, which feems
to be expected from this affembly : and we find
only a mute fcene, as fhort as it is infipid. It
occupies fcarcely one hundred verfes of the poem,
fifty confift of a fpeech which is made in the
affembly, and which in itfelf appears fufficiently
ftrange, after the author has faid,

> " No deputies are there difcreet and bold,
> Our poor remains of freedom to defend."

We are very much aftonifhed at feeing the
only orator who does fpeak in it, is a counfellor
of the Parliament, and that he actually does
claim thofe liberties. So much drynefs, joined
to fuch languor and inaccuracy, is the more
furprifing in a fubject, which, as I before remarked, furnifhed the richeft fund that ever an epic
poet reforted to.

But it feems that Mr. Voltaire, inftead of
feeking to avail himfelf of this richnefs, was
fearful of fhrinking under its weight. Far
from endeavouring to improve it to its full
extent, one would be led to imagine his only
aim was to contract it: he has chalked out
his career, like an infirm man, who, dreading
to find it too long, ufed every means to fhorten it.

We perceive in every page that he is in hafte
to get to the end of his work : inftead of feeking,

as

as the models of the Epopeia have done before
him, by happy illufions, artfully to prolong the
pleafure and admiration of his readers, he thought
he could not get rid of them foon enough. We
may obferve in the fhortnefs of his cantos, in
the ftudied brevity of the few incidents which he
introduces into them, how much he felt oppreffed
under the arduous attempt; the Battle of Ivy
fcarcely contains three hundred verfes, one-third
of which are engaged in the relation of a pathetic
anecdote, but taken elfewhere, that of the young
D'Ailly: it is wholly from Ariofto; and how far
does the copy fall fhort of the original!

But what feems moft unaccountable is, that
writing to a people, among whom the women
have at all times made fo confiderable a figure;
having made them appear with fo much *eclât* in
his tragedies, having chofen for his effay in the
Epopeia an epoch wherein, if they did not fhine
with moft luftre, they acted with more fpirit and
violence than in any other; Mr. Voltaire has
affigned them no part in his poem: for I call
not an epic part the little daily frolic of the 9th
canto, this weak and fervile copy of Taffo, in
which is to be found as little paffion as decency.

Gabriella, that favored beauty, who poffeffed
fo large a fhare not only of the love but the
confidence of Henry IV. and by whom, notwithftanding,

withftanding, he did not always fuffer himfelf to be influenced; Gabriella, who for fome time had reafon to hope, and not without good grounds, of becoming queen; ought to have been one of the principal actreffes on the epic ftage, or not have made her appearance on it at all. It would have been better to have excluded her wholly, than to have made of her a petty adventrefs unknown, and introduced at the end of the poem, to be at once the inftrument and the victim of an artifice, which, having no relation to any thing that had paffed, terminates without leaving any trace behind it.

The predeceffors of the French poet facrificed every thing, hiftory, truth, and probability, in order to procure women of feeling; and he who poffeffed this advantage without any effort, has either neglected it, or knew not how to avail himfelf of it.

Might he not have drawn an interefting part from that famous Duchefs of Montpenfcer, more truly the foul of the League than the Duke of Mayenne; of that implacable woman who always carried fciffars in her pocket, to fhear Henry III. when he was made a monk; who had been one of the principal ornaments of a court, in which beauty ferved fo eminently to pave the way to political depravity, and to infure its fuccefs?

Would

Would not the invocation to love, fupplicating him to lay fnares for the conqueror of Ivy, have been better put into her mouth than into that of Difcord ? Would it have been fo difficult to have made her one of the principal inftruments in the poem, whether fhe had confined her artifices, in endeavouring to make a conqueft of Henry him-felf, or had extended the fnare to feveral officers of the royalifts, and by fuch means to introduce diftruft, difcontent, and treafon into the army which threatened Paris ?

And Mary Stuart, did not hiftory naturally lead the poet to fpeak of the murder of a Queen of France, fo ignobly affaffinated by a vindictive rival ; of a queen whofe misfortunes had fo near a relation to the troubles which with-held Henry from the throne fhe had occupied ? Her beauty, her imprudencies, and her calamities, but too well juftified by her crimes, did they not con-ftitute her a real epic character, and the fubject of an interefting epifode ?

The Earl of Effex too, fo long a favorite of that queen who devoted him to the fcaffold, did not his fate prefent a fit occafion to defcribe the effects of female paffions in general, by bring-ing the Englifh into action, to pourtray theirs in particular ? An event which has furnifhed a fubject for a French tragedy, reprefented every

day,

day, might it not have ferved equally for that of
one canto at leaft in a French epic poem?

But that would have been to depart from
hiftory; Elizabeth never was in love with the Earl
of Effex. She was old.—And what fignifies that?
Achilles perhaps never killed Hector. Hiftory
relates that the fiege of Troy ended in an ac-
commodation difhonorable to the Greeks; and
that the fiege itfelf was far from a very glorious
expedition. Homer wrote to a generation whofe
grandfathers probably affifted at thefe treaties,
and had a fhare in their pretended exploits.
Has he been the lefs lavifh in extolling the
prowefs of his chimerical heroes?

In point of fact, was Henry IV. ever in
England? Was Queen Elizabeth to be defcribed
in love in the epifode? Was love even neceffary
to render her interefting; to defcribe her as a
woman in action, as a living creature, inftead
of a lifelefs buft?

I fay nothing of fo many other characters,
whofe number gives even to the unadorned hiftory of thofe times a dramatic air, fo favorable
to the epic fubject: I will fuppofe that Mr.
Voltaire may be held excufable in not availing
himfelf of them in that extent of which they are
capable, by the powerful aid of fome imaginations;
but how could it happen that the moft fingular
revolutions,

revolutions, the moſt memorable events, ſhould have eſcaped an author who might be ſaid to have them forced on him at every inſtant, and who muſt have been at more trouble to rejeƈt than to make uſe of them.

Whence is it that he has ſaid nothing of Holland; of that admirable monument of human induſtry, of this barrier oppoſed by Deſpair to deſpotiſm; of thoſe natural allies of Henry IV. thoſe irreconcileable and ſucceſsful enemies o Philip II. ? They enter ſo naturally, ſo neceſſarily into the plan of the Henriade, that it muſt have been by an effort of labour and refleƈtion, that they were excluded from it.

How happens it, that not a word is ſaid about the conqueſts of the Portugueſe in Aſia, or of the Spaniards in America; of thoſe immenſe and invaluable dominions, all united under the power of the fortunate Philip, and whoſe treaſures enabled him to ſupport the league in their rebellion?

The novelty of theſe events, the importance of theſe poſſeſſions, and the preponderancy they gave to Spain in the ſcale of power; the riſing rivalſhip of the French, who began to view them with an envious eye, did not all this enter into the ſubjeƈt of a poem, whoſe epocha is fixed at the end of the 16th century, and in which the aƈtors are Frenchmen, Engliſhmen, and Spaniards?

E　　　　　But

But how to pafs from the river Eura to the feas of Mexico and Calicut? From Paris to Vera Cruz, or Goa? How? By an effort of imagination, as Virgil has done in making Æneas and Dido contemporaries, who lived at the diftance of three hundred years from each other; or like Taffo, who ferioufly inlifts as a foldier under Godfrey of Bologne; a Renaldo, that never exifted; and affigns to him a miftrefs, an Armida, no lefs chimerical: or again, like Ariofto, who pleafantly gives to the fabulous Rolando a rival, and a fuccefsful one in the affections of an ideal Chinefe princefs, an Eaftern Shepherd; of whom copies are not uncommon in France, but whofe original is no where to be met with but in the poet's brain. Some means fhould have been found to draw the Indies to Henry's camp, and it does not appear that fuch an attempt would have been impracticable, without even offending againft probability.

The French proteftants had already made more than one enterprize in thefe diftant countries. A Chevalier de Villegagnon had founded in Brafil, in the year 1552, if I miftake not, a colony of proteftants, under the orders and with the affiftance of the Admiral de Colligni. This expedition not proving fuccefsful, fome other navigators of the fame perfuafion had, in 1564,

9   made

made an attempt of the like nature on the coasts of Florida, and were there cruelly massacred by the Spaniards. A detachment of Calvinists, under the command of a Chevalier de Gorgues, had crossed the seas, solely to revenge this murder of their brethren upon a people in other respects distinguished for their generosity, but whose soldiers in this age, and more especially in these newly discovered regions, seem too often to have lost sight of the magnanimity natural to their country.

Might not these martial navigators, attached by birth and religion to Henry IV. and his contemporaries, have made their second appearance with probability in the Henriade, and achieved new exploits against the Spaniards, in relating the past?

Besides, as there were many Castilians and Portuguese in the armies of the League, would it have appeared extraordinary, that some of these should have served under the successors of Cortez or Pizarro? Might they not have had in their suite some Mexicans or Incas? Might not Villegagnon, or the Chevalier de Gorgues, have brought over some natives? When Charles the XIIth. gained the battle of Narva, he made prisoner among the Russians on the borders of the Baltic, a Tartar prince, born near the Palus

Meotides.

Meotides. Might not the French poet have brought into the battle of Ivry, a defcendant of Montezuma or Hufcar, and caufed him to be difarmed by the French monarch? Overpowered by the generofity of his conqueror, the Indian might relate to him the difaflers of his country, and refolve to revenge her wrongs, in taking part with thofe who had juftice on their fide, againft rebels, fupported in their contumacy by her deftroyers.

Might he not have met a mother, a fifter, or a beloved miftrefs, carried off by the Rochellois, in fome of their expeditions againft the new American fettlements of the Spaniards? Their gratitude, their converfion, their happinefs, or their new diftreffes; if the author determined that his new Abradates, in fignalizing his gratitude for the French Cyrus, fhould, like him, be torn from his Panthea; might not all this, have furnifhed matter for an epifode, at once varied, pathetic, and fublime?

Would any reader have accufed the poet on this occafion of boldnefs, or of failing in probability? Would not even reafon itfelf join in applauding the fiction, and does not true philofophy offer here as many, and even more helps to poetry, than the flights of imagination?

In

In thus rejecting beauties which naturally arose out of the subject, has Mr. Voltaire substituted others in their room sufficiently splendid to prevent our regret ? Is it to display his own riches that he seems to have disdained those which his subject offered ? I see in his whole poem but three pieces which deserve the title of episodes; that is, where he has endeavoured to detach himself from history, and to give loose to imagination; the one is the journey to England, in the first canto; the next that to heaven, performed in a dream, in the 7th; and the third, which is a journey likewise, but somewhat different from the other two, is that of the Shepherdess d'Anet, in the 9th canto. Unfortunately if these are not taken from materials supplied by history, they are copied from the Æneid and the Jerusalem, which alone detracts from them a great part of their merit.

I know it will be said, that by an established right every modern writer is at liberty to borrow from those who have gone before him, without incurring censure; Virgil borrowed from Homer, Ariosto and Tasso from Homer and from Virgil; the descent into hell is taken from the Odyssey; Alcida and Armida are drawn after Dido. From this adoption of foreign ideas, when naturalized and embellished in their own language,

E 3 poets

poets have never yet been charged with want of powers, or barrenness of invention.

No, doubtless, when they do embellish them. Thus compare the 6th book of the Æneid, with the invocation of the departed spirits in the Odyssey; and then see if Virgil can be regarded as a copyist. In the Greek poem, Ulysses digs a hole at the mouth of a cave, which has a communication with Tartarus, he pours into it the blood of several victims; the souls then immediately flock thither to drink of it; until they have drunk they recognize no one: and notwithstanding this blindness, and their ætherial nature, the sight of a sword frightens and disperses them; at length when they are admitted to partake of this potent liquid, they recognize Ulysses, and tell him a number of silly, or if you will have it so, ingenious conceits, worthy of all this preparation.

Virgil's descent into hell is as much superior to this gross puerility, as a perfect and finely cut diamond is to the sand in which nature formed it. Are the imitations of Mr. Voltaire equally happy?

The first, which is his visit to London, leads but to an insulated recital; Elizabeth is there for no other end but to hear him, and wish him a good journey; not a single feature is introduced

troduced that bears any relation to the manners
of the Englifh, to the magnificence of London, or to its commerce; to the memorable
reign of Henry VIII. and the manner in which
the daughter of Anna Bullen had acquired the
throne, after being excluded from it. We fee
in this canto, as in the print which ferves for its
frontifpiece, but a clofet, a man feated who is
fpeaking, and a woman feated alfo and attending
to him.

What a falling off is here from the original!
The poet begins with a defcription of the found-
ing of a fuperb city; before he introduces his
hero telling his own ftory, he firft relates that
of the place of which it is natural for him
to fpeak, and of the fovereign who is his au-
ditor. The artifices of Venus have already
prepared the reader for the confequences of this
tale on the unfortunate queen, and indeed attention leads her to affection. She indulges a
flame for a hero who fo gracefully relates his
misfortunes. She gives way to a paffion which
appears in itfelf innocent, and which is even
fanctioned by policy; and fhe falls a victim to it.
The defcription of her love, of her defpair, and
the cataftrophe with which it concludes, is at
once a mafter-piece of fentiment and poetry,
which has never yet been equalled in any language.

E 4   Laftly,

Lastly, By an effort of genius which cannot be sufficiently admired, this piece, which abstractedly considered, and stripped of every other merit than the perfection of the picture itself, would have excited the constant wonder and the admiration of men of every country, was to the Romans interwoven with one of the most remarkable events of their history: it accounted for the origin of that irreconcileable hatred, which had so long prevailed between the descendants of Dido and of Æneas, between Rome and Carthage; and in some measure justifies the ruin of the latter—crushed at length by the power of her more fortunate rival. Every man of letters knows, and can recite by heart, those verses which will retain their novelty to the end of time,

Rise some avenger of our Libyan blood,
With fire and sword—pursue the perjur'd brood;
Our arms, our seas, our shores oppofed to theirs,
And the fame hate defcend on all our heirs.

DRYDEN.

Does the feeble French imitation retain the least trace of these beauties, and more especially the last, which, by a singular similarity of circumstance, should have presented itself to the poet? Is not the rivalship between England and France, between London and Paris, nearly the same?

Was

Was not this the place to have invented a reaſon equally ſpecious to explain why the ſtraits of Ca-lais, which ſeparate the two countries by the in-tervention of ſo ſmall a ſpace, ſhould have made ſuch an immenſe difference in the minds of their inhabitants.

The kings were then in amity, it is true, but the kingdoms were not; beſides, the buſineſs was not to copy this effort of genius in the Æ-neid, but to equal it, to ſubſtitute another in its ſtead, which, notwithſtanding this temporary agreement of the two people, ſhould bear as pointed an alluſion to their ſecret and hereditary diſpoſition towards each other. With ſo ad-mirable a model in his view, and while pur-poſing to imitate it, Mr. Voltaire has reduced his peaceful conference between the ſceptered ambaſſador, and the daughter of Henry the Eighth; to mere compliments, portraits, and antitheſes.

There is, perhaps, a ſtill greater difference between the dream, wherein a ſainted king be-comes the guide of Henry the Fourth, and the ſubterraneous paſſage in which a Sybil performs the like ſervice to Eneas.—In the ſame degree that the deſcription of the Latin poet is grand, ſimple, affecting, clear, and ſkilfully interſperſed with a variety of philoſophic, hiſtoric, mytho-logical,

logical, and moral matter, that of the French is
hurried, monotonous, and obfcure.

Virgil, when the nature of the place is too
difmal, is careful to relieve the gloom by the
fucceffive meeting of Palinurus, Caron, Deipho-
bus and Dido : there is not even a defcription of
Tartarus, which is not animated by painting and
poetry, alike deftined to immortality, as in that of
the unhappy Tytyus;

> A rav'nous vulture in his opened fide
> Her crooked beak, and cruel talons try'd :
> Still for the growing liver digg'd his breaft,
> The growing liver ftill fupply'd the feaft :
> Still are his entrails fruitful to their pains,
> Th' immortal hunger lafts, th' immortal food remains.
>   DRYDEN.

or of that celebrated reprobate who calls aloud,

> Learn righteoufnefs, and dread th' avenging deities.
>   DRYDEN.

and many more with which this piece abounds.

The geography of the country is accurately
defcribed agreeably to the pagan mythology;
the two travellers firft pafs over the river Ache-
ron, then traverfe the entrance into hell, in
which there is rather privation of happinefs than
actual mifery. They then arrive at Tartarus
itfelf, in which are atrocious criminals, and real
punifhments; and, laftly, they reach the Elyfian
Fields,

Fields, where futurity is unfolded to them on the borders of Lethe. All these distant regions were in effect placed by the fable near each other, and under the same power. The poet is at the same time a majestic philosopher, and an accurate delineator of the religious opinions which prevailed in his days.

But in the Henriade, the two kings immediately ascend into heaven, to assist at the judgment of souls; from whence they are transported in a whirlwind into a chaos, where is hell according to the poet, and purgatory according to the saint; near at hand is paradise, and at the end of paradise the palace of the Fatal Sisters. We comprehend nothing of this expedition: it is not conformable to our religious ideas; there is no reason to suppose that the author meant to give it as a system of his own: what is it then? Certainly this blending together of terms and ideas, half pagan and half christian, can never be deemed a beauty, in which we can neither trace the doctrine of one of these persuasions, nor find any of the pleasing illusions which accompany the other. It may even be said that the morality of the latter is far more rigid. Virgil places in that part of hell called Tartarus, not only those guilty of sacrilege, tyrants, and traitors who have sold their country, but voluptuous epicures,

epicures, and, what is much more rigid, thofe
avaricious wretches who have not difpenfed a
part of their riches among their relations; while
the French poet piteoufly exclaims,

.——————oh! ye fons of eafe,
Muft tender fpirits dwell in climes like thefe;
Ye who on flowery couches pafs'd away
The tranquil moments of life's ufeful day.

That we may be the better able to conceive
the prodigious diftance between the original and
his imitator, we muft above all bring thofe paffages together wherein by a fingular concurrence
of circumftances the two poets had precifely the
fame things to fay, the fame loffes to deplore,
and where confequently the modern might, and
even ought, to have taken the ancient for his
model.

In the Æneid we fee a young Marcellus, in
the Henriade a young duke of Burgundy, both
born to a throne, both affording the faireft hopes,
alike untimely fnatched from their families and
their country, extolled alike in the poems by
the founders of thofe families, whofe glory it is
fuppofed they would have proved; and finally,
both recently brought again into exiftence, to
anfwer the purpofe of the poets: fince the duke
died in 1712, and the Henriade, at that time
called

called the League, appeared in 1723; but this is all the fimilarity between them. The lamentations of Anchifes are natural, affecting, and expreffive of an enthufiafm at once grand and mournful.

'The gods too high had rais'd the Roman ftate;
Were but their gifts as permanent, as great.
What groans of men fhall fill the Martian field.
How fierce a blaze his flaming pile fhall yield!
What fun'ral pomp fhall floating Tyber fee,
When rifing from his bed, he views the fad folemnity!
No youth fhall equal hopes of glory give,
No youth afford fo great a caufe to grieve:
The Trojan honor, and the Roman boaft,
Admir'd when living, and ador'd when loft!
Mirror of ancient worth, in early youth,
Undaunted faith, inviolable truth!
No foe unpunifh'd in the fighting field,
Shall dare thee foot to foot, with fword and fhield;
Much lefs in arms oppofe thy matchlefs force,
When thy fharp fpurs fhall urge thy foaming horfe.
Ah, cou'dft thou break thro' fate's fevere decree,
A new Marcellus fhall arife in thee!
Full canifters of fragrant lilies bring,
Mix'd with the purple rofes of the fpring:
Let me with fun'ral flowers his body ftrow,
This gift which parents to the children owe,
This unavailing gift, at leaft I'may beftow.

DRYDEN.

This is the language of a poet; let us now hear his imitator.

What

What princely youth draws near, whose manly face,
United majesty and sweetness grace?
See how unmov'd—Oh heavens! what sudden shade
Conceals the graces which his form display'd!
Death flutters round; health, beauty, all is gone,
He falls, just ready to ascend the throne:.
Heaven form'd him all that's truly just and good,
Descended Bourbon from thy royal blood.
Oh gracious God! shall fate but shew mankind
A flower so sweet, and virtues so refin'd:
What could a soul so gen'rous not obtain?
What joys wou'd France experience from his reign?
Produc'd and nurtur'd by his fostering hand,
Fair peace and plenty had enrich'd the land.
Each day some new beneficence had brought:
Oh how shall Gallia weep! alarming thought!
When one dark silent sepulchre contains
The son's, the mother's, and the sire's remains.

What a difference! Does Anchises amuse himself in saying of Marcellus that he was a transi-
tory flower? Does he apply the epithet of au-
gust to that blood which springing from the posterity of his son, was of consequence his own?
Does he call the most upright of the Romans a
young man who never was to fill the throne?
An epithet the more singular in the French author, as he had before said of Lewis the Twelfth,
that that monarch,

Rul'd our realm with justice at his side:

and that of course it is difficult to be more just.
Does he content himself with saying he would

have

have loved his people? An eulogium fo weak after this verfe,

Each day fome new beneficence had brought:

an eulogium, moreover, which is but a repetition, fince the poet has already faid, fome few lines above, of the cardinal of Amboife, that

To him alone was Gallia's homage dear,
To him alone her homage was fincere.

And, laftly, let us fee if the ancient Trojan more drily breaks off in a cold exclamation on the afflicting image of a tomb, and in an anecdote unintelligible without a note or a previous knowledge of the fact, that this whole family became extinct at once. Anchifes does not complain to the gods of their hard treatment of Marcellus; he accufes them of being jealous of him. " The fates will but fhew him to the " earth; fathers of heaven! Rome, had fhe " preferved him, would have appeared to you " too powerful." If he fpeaks of a tomb, it is that he may join with it an image which gives it animation, and renders the idea affecting and foft. " With what regret fhall the field of Mars " refound! what tears, oh Tyber! as thou paffeft " the verge of that tomb newly erected on thy " banks, fhalt thou fee fhed!" It is not at the

expence of the great men of his line that he
praifes his young defcendant. " Never fhall
" child have afforded fuch grounds for the moft
" fanguine hopes, *nec puer.*" It appears to
me that there is contained in thefe words an admirable delicacy, far from making him eclipfe
the ancient heroes; his greateft merit will be to
poffefs their virtues and fidelity; " heu pietas,
" heu prifca fides !" At length, he thus addreffes
him : " Unhappy boy ! fhould'ft thou be able
" to vanquifh the cruelty of thy fate, thou will'ft
" prove a real Marcellus—give me lilies in
" abundance, that I may cover his dear fhade
" with flowers, that I may at leaft offer to it
" this unavailing homage." This is the fpeech
of Anchifes, as far as the weaknefs of the idiom,
and my own want of power enable me to render
it. We may difcover through it the expreffion
and the poetry of the original: accordingly,
though we are neither Auguftus nor Octavia,
and though eighteen centuries are fince elapfed,
this piece forces tears from us.—Can its feeble
copy do the like? The epifode of Gabrielle,
when compared with thofe of Dido and Armida,
is no lefs inferior in the detail of circumftances,
and is moreover effentially defective in itfelf, becaufe the hero is debafed. Every thing concurs
to degrade Henry the Fourth in his unfortunate

5   adventure

adventure with Anet, as it is reprefented in the poem.

I have already called it a trick ; and what other name can we give to this ftrange incident, or the manner in which it is conducted, and in which it finifhes? to that fudden and tender reconciliation unexpectedly produced through the intervention of Difcord to this amour, which arofe from chance, and which vanifhes like the intrigues of a campaigner, the day after its birth? The reader who reflects finds here but one embarraf-ment, which is, to determine whether the hero is lefs when he quits his miftrefs, than when lying at her feet.

Dido conceives a paffion for a ftranger; but with what fkill is her weaknefs conducted ! how well does fhe appear juftified ! how many inte-refting events are produced from it ! The object of her affection is a hero, and the fon of the goddefs of love; it is under the appearance of generofity that this paffion infinuates itfelf into her heart; Æneas is as unfortunate as he is ami-able; his eloquence finifhes what his adverfity, his form, and the power of his mother had be-gun ; nor was it till a moft pathetic tale had dif-played his virtues in their full luftre, that fhe wholly yields herfelf up to the paffion with which

F he

he infpired her. Befides, fhe defended herfelf
againft it: fhe for a long time oppofed to this rifing
attachment, her ancient refolution to contract no
new alliance, the remembrance of her firft hufband, a regard to her own glory : nothing is
omitted which might ferve to give proofs of
her virtue, and to render her weaknefs excufable.

And at length to accomplifh her fall, it was
neceffary that her mind fhould be previoufly
difpofed to tendernefs, by that kind of emotion
which accompanies the pomp of a fplendid fefti-
val; Juno and Venus muft concert together to
overcome her refiftance. To effect her overthrow, all the merits of a hero, all the influence
of two powerful divinities, all thofe incidents
which, taking the mind by furprife, lead to the
difcovery of paffion, muft combine together. And
what grandeur, what poetry, what truth is there
not in the general reprefentation, and in each
particular detail of this unhappy attachment!

Taffo has likewife made his hero in love. He
has defcribed him for a moment buried in pleafure : but when Rinaldo abandons himfelf to the
careffes of Armida, independent of the power
of magic, by which he is captivated, it is in a
time of exile and leifure, at a time when his
mind was inflamed with juft refentment againft
his general, and when an order which he could

not

not avenge caufed his abfence from the chriftian army.

Let it be remembered too, that it is a ftranger, an enchantrefs, free and miftrefs of herfelf, by whom he is fought after, the triumph which he gains over her can neither tarnifh his own repu tation, nor affect the interefts of his party; on the contrary, he is ftill victorious, and almoft an hero while fuffering himfelf to be enflaved: it is as we may fay honor, which gives him up to love. In fhort, he is not only in the flower of youth, and confequently in the feafon when errors are moft readily excufed, but the paffion which he infpires, and which he himfelf feels, continues long enough to acquire a fort of dig- nity: for love becomes ennobled by conftancy. A confiderable interval elapfes, and a variety of events take place, between the period which fhews him enervated by pleafure, and that which reftores him to glory: his tranfports are not be- gun and concluded in the fame canto.

But Henry, in a mature age, with the expe- rience of misfortune, in the moft critical mo- ment of his affairs, delivers himfelf up to the firft appearance of pleafure: at a time, when after gaining a battle, his abfence might caufe him to lofe the fruits of it, he abfents himfelf without reflection; and for what? to feduce a

young

young perfon whofe innocence he ought, efpecially after his journey to heaven, to have re-
fpected; and what is ftill more fcandalous, and
ftill more inconceivable, this young perfon is the
daughter of one of his old officers, who at the
very moment is hazarding his life in his fervice.

It is the author who informs us,

——————fhe waits her fire,
Who faithful to our kings, and old in arms,
Had follow'd Henry's enfigns in the field.

In return, the great Henry goes to fee his daughter, feduces and abandons her, and all this in an
inftant of time.

But is that the fact? no; firft, as I have already faid, Gabrielle in hiftory is nothing lefs
than a fimple fhepherdefs, eafily feduced and
foon forgotten: but were it even the truth, that
was not an anecdote that fhould have been feized
and introduced into an epic poem; on the contrary, it fhould have been wholly fuppreffed, or
metaphorfed by an effort of the imagination.
The charms of Armida are no where fuffered to
operate to the prejudice of Rinaldo's fame. This
artifice fhould have been imitated. Were it
neceffary to fpeak of the weaknefs of a hero, it
fhould have been covered with a veil, which
would have refcued it from ignominy.

9   It

It appears true then, that the author of the Henriade has not embellifhed his fubject, that he has even voluntarily weakened it, by neglecting to avail himfelf of thofe beauties which naturally arife out of it; and inftead of that mixture of fiction which in other epic poems, whofe names have been confecrated by time, furnifhes the ground of a career at once fo rapid, and notwithftanding fo well fuftained, fo varied, and fo interefting; we find in this but a frigid monotony; we admire, indeed, the fine verfes with which it often abounds, efpecially in the level and defcriptive parts, but the events neither excite intereft or paffion. In a word, if I may be permitted to give my opinion, the Henriade is rather a differtation in rhyme, an ornamented treatife in verfe, on the latter half of the fixteenth century, than a poem.

But it will be faid, the author could do no more; he was deprived of one grand refource, open to all his predeceffors, that of the marvellous: our religion forbids thofe fictions which paganifm authorifed, and our manners fuch as were tolerated by the cuftoms of chivalry. The Italians, who have immortalifed Armida and Rolando, were enabled to fubftitute the wonders of magic and the illufions of enchantment, inftead of the deities of Greece and Rome: this

the

the name of his hero, the proximity of the time, and the progress of letters in our age, denied to Mr. Voltaire. Assuredly an Ismeno would have made but a poor figure by the side of the duke of Mayenne; we should have condemned the poet if he had, like Tasso, enchanted by a sorcerer all the trees of the forest of Bondy, in order to prevent the siege of Paris; and although the charming d'Estrèes was, perhaps, in reality more beautiful than the supposed Armida, the Parisian author would not have been excused had he built, by the stroke of a wand, a beautiful magic palace in the midst of d'Anet's park, in which Henry should have been immured within walls of adamant.

I acknowledge it: neither is it these fairy tales which have established the success of the Jerusalem and the Orlando. On the contrary, they would have proved their downfall, or have sunk them into contempt, without those just representations, without those affecting and grand situations, with which the skill of the artists has embellished these chimeras. What father le Bossu ridiculously enough calls the machinery, that is, the intervention of supernatural beings, I do not think at all necessary to the epopéia.

Virgil

Virgil has adopted it, but it is likewife the weakeft part of his poem. The gods of Homer do not caft a damp on the Iliad, becaufe they are but men: they have their language and paffions, and moreover enter for nothing into the fineft parts of this revered poem.

They are not to be found in the parting of Hector and Andromache, nor in that nervous fcene, fo fraught with varied eloquence, between the deputies of the Greeks, and Achilles refufing them his affiftance; they form no part of the adventure of Patroclus, nor of that fcene, perhaps ftill more beautiful than any of the reft, wherein Priam comes to kifs the hand ftained with the blood of his fon: we connot confider as an intervention of a divinity, the fubaltern part which Mercury performs. It is not, therefore, the marvellous which conftitutes the merit of thefe models in the art of relating, defcribing, and moving; but thefe pieces are interefting, becaufe they prefent nothing but what is natural. In fairy tales the marvellous is profufely introduced; accordingly they intereft not: far from the epic poem not being able to difpenfe with gods, with forcerers, or intellectual beings, however perfonified; I am perfuaded, on the contrary, that the only means of equalling at prefent the models handed down to us in this fpecies of

F 4

writing,

writing, and to form others equal to them, would be to set aside these puerile and superfluous expedients.

True epic fictions should consist of events skilfully conceived, artfully arranged, and happily described. These poems are romances in verse; interest accordingly in these, as in romances, should give birth to grand passions, happily seized and ably developed; to incidents, regularly connected and well related; to episodes, which arise without constraint, and interwoven in such a manner as to prolong the action of the poem, without suspending its effect, or weakening its force; in short, an address, a fecundity to multiply situations capable of calling forth the passions, traits which depict the hero but by means of facts, in which they are seen to act, and not of words, which only discover the author.

This is the truce machinery of the Æneid, the Iliad, the Jerusalem, the Orlando, &c. and not the gods and bugbears, which, if they stood alone, would have been abandoned, with Tom Thumb and Blue Beard, to children. These fictions exist independent of a change of manners, or the variations of prejudice in doctrines or in government; they are allied to the heart, which is always the same; to that natural disposition by which we are always led to admire

what

what is great, to efteem what is ingenious, and to fympathife with what is pathetic. This is the true marvellous, which has fucceeded in all ages, and which offers to true poetry a thoufand times more refources than all the witchcrafts and enchantments in the world.

Even fuppofing, with father le Boffu, a machinery ftill neceffary, it is not the impoffibility of fupplying one which conftitutes the weaknefs of the Henriade, fince the author, like his predeceffors, has availed himfelf of this help in adopting their inventions; but he has been as unfortunate in this as in his other attempts.

For inftance, we fee Difcord perfonified in his work, as in the Orlando; fhe is even a perfonage of much greater confequence; in the Italian poem fhe plays but a fubaltern and momentary part, whereas fhe is the foul, the mover, and the entire machinery of the French one. To appreciate the imagination of the two poets, we need but compare the effects refpectively produced by them from this refource, which they have in common chofen.

In the Henriade, Difcord is perfonified in the fourth canto, and fhe appears for herfelf alone; d'Aumale is expofed in a fally, fhe trembles to lofe him.

As

As barb'rous as the fiend, she fears to lose
A life so needful to her, she to his succor flies,
And 'gainst surrounding enemies his breast defends
With her vast iron impenetrable + shield.

He escapes from thence; she departs to Rome
in search of Policy to come and corrupt the
Sorbonne, an office it appears to me she was
herself very capable of executing; she makes a
second journey to hell, to engage Fanaticism to
come and prepare the assassination of Henry the
Third, a function which appears neither above
nor beneath her own power; she then for a moment animates the Sixteen, and finishes with an
invocation to Love to come and enslave Henry
the Fourth.

In all this, excepting the protection which she
affords to d'Aumale, and her league with Love,

---

4 It is singular enough that Mr. Voltaire, fearful of giving too much into the marvellous, from a regard to the philosophy of his age, has armed Discord with a shield, which
Homer himself would never have done. This poet, an exact
observer of proprieties, never gives this sort of armour but
to those deities whose attributes it in some sort coincided
with; to Jupiter, the supreme god; to Minerva, and to
Mars, the peculiar divinities of war. Neptune, Apollo,
and Mercury have no shield; when they wish to engage in
the field they borrow the Ægis, or clothe themselves in the
armour of ordinary combatants: a proof, in my opinion,
that even in his enthusiasm Homer did not lose sight of his
good sense, and that he hazarded nothing without reflection.

which

which are not two very great or marvellous in-cidents, the hiſtory is didactically followed. The Diſcord of Mr. Voltaire is to be found equally with P. de Thou as in the Henriade : this pre-tended fury is there no longer a poetical perſon-age, but a name given to the ſpirit which ani-mated the league and its partiſans.

This name too is as ill imagined as it is ill applied : with equal propriety might the poet have perſonified Ambition, Revenge, &c. and have aſſigned them the ſame parts which he has to Diſcord. In the conduct of the latter we perceive nothing characteriſtic of her name, or rather on the contrary ſhe belies it ; for, in-ſtead of being employed in cauſing diviſion, her ſole care is to promote union.

It is true, that the object of the union thus effected, is to produce miſchief, but this ſigni-fies not ; to juſtify her title ſhe ſhould have ac-compliſhed this by diſſeminating diſorder, miſ-truſt, and hatred : the object of her manœuvres in the party of Henry, ſhould be to detach his friends from his intereſts, and to incite them againſt each other, inſtead of being con-fined as they are, to ſtrengthen the union of his enemies.

Would you behold a real Diſcord, a Diſcord poetical and active, ſee one delineated by Arioſto.

A

A cloud of infidels in arms, and in perfect union, threaten Chriftendom under the command of Agramant, the Agamemnon of thefe new Greeks. God employing fecondary caufes for the prefervation of his church, fends an angel in fearch of Difcord, and orders her to perplex thefe mifcreants; to excite fuch divifions in the troops as fhall confound and defeat their enterprifes. The angel feeks her, and finds her in a chapter of monks, (obferve that the Orlando is an hero-comic poem, a fpecies of which I fhall fhortly fpeak,) he announces his commiffion to her, fhe departs, and alights on the infidel army.

The camp is immediately filled with diffentions, difputes, and quarrels of every kind: the moft important arife among the principal warriors, who determine to fettle them by fingle combat. As there are four whofe mutual interefts are involved in the moft complicated perplexity, they are forced to draw lots to know who is to begin the battle. The lot falls on Mandricard and Rodomant. The day is fixed: whatever concern thefe diforders, and ftill more this mode of appeafing them, may caufe to the great Agramant, he is forced to confent.

All the cuftoms of knight-errantry are pourtrayed and defcribed with the greateft fplendor by the poet. Two tents are prepared at the extremities

extremities of the camp, to which the combatants refpectively repair, each with his fquires, whofe office it is to prefent him with the different pieces of his armour. One of the fquires in giving Mandricard his fword, which is that of Rolando, recognifes it; he had formerly vowed to conquer this fword likewife, and determines to keep it. A great difpute enfues. Roger, one of the four knights whofe combat was delayed by the event of the lots, renews his pretenfions, and will no longer refpect the order agreed on, becaufe it was infringed by a new competitor. Mandricard challenges both foes at the fame time: they all go out in a rage, ready to attack each other; and here are already three duels for one.

Agramant aftonifhed at the uproar, haftens thither with his Neftor, the old Marfillus: whilft they are feeking the means of reconciliation, a dreadful tumult is heard in the other tent. Rodomont was ready to mount his charger, of which he had gained poffeffion after many adventures, when one of the fquires examining the harnefs of the fiery fteed, perceives him to be his dear Creamface, an excellent horfe, which had been formerly ftolen from him, and fince the lofs of which he had fworn to go on foot till he fhould find him again. He inftantly feifes the bridle, makes

oath

oath that he will never again quit it, and draws his fword in fupport of his right: hence proceed mutual reproaches, blows, and a horrible tumult.

Agramánt leaves Marfillus to reftrain one of the tents within bounds, and returns haftily to the other, followed by a great number of the principal officers of the army, all like him much furprifed at this new mifchance. Among thefe is the haughty Marphifa, an invincible Amazon, arrived lately in the Moorifh camp, with the fole d:fi $_{3}$n of challenging the knight-errants in the army of Charlemagne. Hearing the ftolen horfe fpoken of, fhe recollects being acquainted with his owner, and that on the fame day when he was thus cheated by a knave, fhe herfelf loft a rich and valuable fword. She is much furprifed to find the thief in the fuite of d'Agremant, who, to reward him, has made him a king: fhe falls on the crowned plunderer, drags him to the neck of the horfe to hang him, and challenges Agramant himfelf, if he interpofes his authority. This completes the general confufion; and all the interefted parties having their troops in the army and their party in the council, the diforder that muft refult from thefe divifions in the hoft of Charlemagne's enemies may be eafily conceived.

This

This is what is achieved by Difcord in the Orlando en paffant, where fhe is but an epifodic and momentary perfonage: this is what Ariofto has produced from nothing, what fcarcely occupies in his work a quarter of a canto. I know not if in all the ancient and modern poets there is to be found a paffage which gives ftronger proofs of genius and imagination.

Cervantes has imitated it with confiderable art in his Don Quixote; but Cervantes is but a copyift. How weak and inefficient appears, the profing Difcord of the French author, after the active one of the Italian! It is not then owing to the revolution which has taken place in our manners and religion, that the Henriade is fo far inferior, even in point of machinery, to the poems which have gone before it.

It abounds with very fine portraits I have acknowledged; but I repeat, thefe cold inanimate images freeze the poem: other epic works have their portraits likewife, but they refult from the action of their heroes; they are not hung up and faftened motionlefs to a wall, till the eye of the fpectator fhall happen to catch them: it is the reader, who having feen the characters in action, figures them to himfelf, their forms, their figure, and phyfiognomy are prefent to his imagination,

gination, he has previoufly conceived an idea of
their character.

Does Ariofto wifh to difplay the greatnefs of
foul, the generofity, the haughty heroifm of a
knight, who is above all things apprehenfive left
he fhould be fufpected of feeking to avail himfelf of unfair advantages in battle, who wifhes
to be indebted to his prowefs alone for his fame;
he does not lofe time in meafuring terms and
fonorous verfes, metaphyfically to defcribe what
paffes in the breaft of the warrior; he produces
on the fcene, Roger armed by the enchanter
Atlant with a marvellous fhield compofed of a
fingle diamond, whofe luftre at once ftrikes the
beholders blind, and deprives them of all power
of motion. This is an imitation of the head
of Medufa, but what follows is an imitation of
no one.

Roger has taken the fhield becaufe it is impenetrable, and becaufe the laws of chivalry do
not deny to valour any help that it may derive
from the fuperior temper or folidity of arms;
but he carefully covers it with a veil, in order
that he may by no means be indebted to its other
property.

In the midft of a fcuffle however, wherein he is
infulted by ftrangers, who attack him feveral of
them together, a blow is ftruck on the veil, which

tears

tears it, the fatal light manifefts itfelf; the whole troop in a moment fall motionlefs, and the herd finds himfelf out of danger.

But difdaining a premature help, which feems to leave his courage in doubt, he perceives a deep well, into which he haftens to plunge the burning fhield, and precipitates it before him, that he may no longer be fufpected of relying more on the affiftance of magic than his own fword. This trait from Orlando is doubtlefs fine even in a fabulous hero; and what prevented Mr. Voltaire from creating the like ones under real names?

Whatever had a tendency to elevate the mind; to foften, to furprife, or to intereft, has been eagerly adopted by the epic poets, even among the moderns who preceded Mr. Voltaire; they have in fome fort prodigally dealt them out with equal profufion and fuccefs. Sometimes it is from incidents arifing in the common order of events, which are rendered extraordinary by aids derived from genius alone; at others the circumftances, though in themfelves romantic, are introduced with fuch attention to probability, and pourtrayed in a manner fo pathetic, that the heart is captivated before the underftanding can find time for cenfure.

G   Thus

Thus that a jealous woman fhould be driven to reproaches, threats, and even actual violence againft a rival, is what often happens, and requires no great effort of the mind to conceive; but that fhe fhould enjoy the fatisfaction of feeing this rival expofed to the danger of lofing her life by the hands of that lover who is thought unfaithful, or of depriving him of exiftence by her own; that fuch a one as fhe fhould enjoy this fcene with delight, and that it fhould be a probable confequence of contempt, is an interefting fiction, well adapted to the epopeia which is to be found in Ariofto.

That a lover by another miftake, rendered equally probable, fhould have the misfortune to kill his miftrefs, while he fuppofes himfelf engaging and conquering his mortal foe, is a fiction lefs natural indeed, but equally diftrefing, and calculated to move every heart: this is to be found in the Jerufalem, when Tancred takes Clorinda for Argant, whofe armour fhe wore, and it is there admirably managed. Again, a lover equally delicate and faithful, but excluded by the relations of his miftrefs, a celebrated warrior, is informed that, with the view of repulfing all his rivals, and infuring him her hand, fhe has formed the refolution of beftowing it only upon him who can vanquifh her in the lifts; that, by a con-

concurrence of extraordinary circumftances, he finds himfelf compelled to maintain his combat under the name, the arms, and for the benefit of a ftranger who had preferved his life; fo that if he is overcome, he is liable to the fufpicion of having betrayed the confidence of his bene-factor; and thus become, in a double point of view, unworthy of his miftrefs; and, if he proves victor, it muft be to throw her into the arms of another. This again is a fiction, which interefts and affects the reader in a moft fenfible degree; and it is the ground of the epifode of prince Leon at the conclufion of the Orlando. All the fituations, it is true, arife from the miftakes juftified by the cuftoms of chivalry. The vizors of the helmets in thofe times concealed the combatants, who were not otherwife diftin-guifhable but by particular marks, as their horfes, their armour, &c. and the cuftom of fighting with the face uncovered, which preceded our own of braving lead, iron, and fire, with the entire body expofed, deprives our poets of this refource, fo fertile in beauty; but how many others remain open to them? With how many models of a different nature do the authors I have enumerated furnifh them?

The Henriade, as I have before remarked, has but one fingle amour, an amour which

G 2 occupies

occupies but a fingle canto, which does not depend on the poem, an amour which degrades
the hero without exalting the miftrefs, which
afflicts the mind, without affecting the heart.
Ariofto has twenty, all varied, all pleafing, all
interwoven in interefting epifodes, related to the
principal action of the poem, and adapted to
the feveral characters of the perfonages; and in
defcribing which the poet fometimes difcovers
the tendereft fenfibility, at others the moft fterling humor.

Ifabella and Zerbin are models of honor and
delicacy. Roger is more ardent, and Brada-
mante more empaffioned, but always decent.
Mendriard is a libertine, and the beautiful Do-
ralixa precifely what a woman fhould be to prefer fuch a lover. Rodomonte abandoned by her,
plays a ridiculous part: his difafter is comic,
and he is, notwithftanding, not difparaged by it.
Alcine, Angelica, Medor, and feveral others,
throw into the vaft field of the Orlando an inexhauftible variety; there is no mind, no heart,
but may find materials whereon to exercife the
fenfibility they poffefs, whether derived from
their natural organization, or from a tafte developed and perfected by reflection.

Taffo is lefs fertile: he is always grave, always
majeftic; but, as I faid before, the tendernefs
which

which breathes through every page of his work, tempers its elevation.

In the Æneid Dido is but an epifode, but how beautiful a one! How foft is the beginning, how animated its conclufion! In the Iliad Brifeis is a fort of outwork without action; but Andromache occupies a grand place in the picture; and this fcene of conjugal love, depicted with the moft expreffive traits, disfigures none of the paffions with which it is furrounded, nor is itfelf weakened by them. In the Henriade we perceive none of thefe beauties, nor even any thing which can furnifh us with the leaft trace of them.

After thefe obfervations, what then are the remaining merits of this work? Firft, as I have obferved, the title of epic, which is a very inconfiderable one, and the ftill more effential excellence of containing fome very fine verfes, and fome portraits admirably drawn; of collecting together in the text and in the notes annexed to it, the principal events of an epocha ever memorable to the French nation; of furnifhing to thofe amongft them who have the charge of educating youth, fome details, which they may compare in their language with the fine defcriptions taken from the poets of antiquity. This will not prevent the work from exhibiting the inferiority of

G 3

its

its author, and proves only, that amid the variety of mental powers which nature had profufely endowed him with, fhe had at leaft refufed him one.

In other refpects I am inclined to think, that it is rather owing to the precipitation of Mr. Voltaire's friends than to himfelf, that we fhould impute the imperfections of the Henriade, and even its exiftence. He had, as it is well known, conceived the plan, and made his firft fketch of it, at an age when it is difficult to conceive that he fhould be able to do juftice to fuch an attempt, efpecially while dividing his time, and devoting his attention in the manner he did, to all the fubjects of literature. The fociety he then lived in was compofed of friends rather enlightened than rational, poffeffed of more delicacy than paffion, delivered up to a philofophy proper enough for the cultivation of tafte, but not calculated to roufe the imagination, and valuing themfelves on a peculiar mode of thinking on every fubject.

The draught of the Henriade, under the name of the League, was very highly applauded by them; they found in it fome lively paffages againft the priefthood which pleafed them, and fome fine verfes which they admired with ftill more reafon: they were not repelled by the coldnefs of their principles.

principles. Inftead of giving the young author fuch wholefome advice as would have induced him to abandon the defign, they loaded him with fuch eulogiums as induced him to commit it to the prefs, not only before the coloring was complete, but before any thing was fettled either in the defign or in the execution.

Thefe praifes thus lavifhly beftowed, caft an illufion before the public; and even the author himfelf, fortified by thefe againft his own internal conviction, has all his life long labored to polifh his fketch, but he never thought of improving or enlarging the plan of it, and had he conceived the defign, perhaps he might not have been able to execute it. He would conftantly have preferred the more eafy labor of the theatre, and the numberlefs more pleafing occupations which he had formed, to that profound meditation, and thofe laborious efforts neceffary to form the plan of a good epic poem, and ftill more to amend that of a bad one.

OF

OF

Mr. VOLTAIRE's

SECOND EPIC POEM,

NEARLY about the fame time that Mr. Voltaire was thus occupied on the ferious epopeia, he adventured to try the burlefque. We find in the hiftory of France a fecond epocha, almoft fimilar to that which has been the fubject of our remarks: that is, the reign of Charles the Seventh; the events and the two monarchs bear a like affinity to each other.

Charles and Henry were both brave, both amiable and indulgent; they alike intermingled pleafures and bufinefs, love and war; both were profcribed in their own dominions, and had to wreft from their fubjects, fupported in rebellion by foreigners, their own territories, which were likewife the fame. It was the care of each, when fettled on the throne, to re-eftablifh order and plenty in their provinces, that had been fo

long

long in a ftate of defolation. Laftly, they both met with a melancholy and premature death; the one perifhed with hunger, for fear of being poifoned by his fon; the other fell by the hand of one of his fubjects.

The firft difference we perceive between them is, that religion, which occafioned all the misfortunes of Henry, had no influence on the affairs of Charles; and a fecond is, the furprifing event which diftinguifhes the reign of the latter, in the fuccour he derived from the Maid, furnamed d'Orleans, becaufe her firft exploit was that of making the Englifh raife the fiege of that town.

If one of thefe reigns has been deemed worthy of the epopeia, and capable of furnifhing the fubject of an heroic poem, why fhould not the fecond be entitled to the like honor? Joan of Arc, without doubt, fighting for her country, equalling the moft renowned warriours in valour and fuccefs, carries nothing ridiculous in it. The Clorindas, the Marphifas, the Bradamantas, the Camillas are not fo, and it may be fairly queftioned if they ever equalled the fhepherdefs of Vancouleurs.

The daftardly cruelty, which not being able to conquer, was capable of avenging itfelf on her courage by condemning her to a barbarous death, might

have

have fupplied a moft affecting epifode: I know not if I am miftaken, but it appears to me that the fubverfion of France, and its re eftablifhment under the father of Louis the Eleventh, opened a new field to the epopeia, and prefented refources which might have interefted readers of every nation, and from ftronger motives thofe of that country in particular.

Unhappily, a man void of genius has undertaken this fine fubject, and failed in the attempt: it has therefore, after the manner of the French, been haftily confidered as impracticable. Becaufe Chapelain has not fucceeded, it has been fettled that no one elfe could. Mr. Voltaire himfelf fomewhere treats the idea of confidering it ferioufly as abfurd; and fo well was he perfuaded of this, that, after having dared to cope with Virgil in the ferious line, he now propofed imitating the moft humorous part of Ariofto, and made choice of this fubject as a canvas adapted to receive this light bordering, and, under the title of the Pucelle, given us an exact parody of the Henriade.

This work has had a great run. The youthful part of its readers have been feduced by the licentious pictures with which it abounds, and fome voluptuous images which are to be found in it: even connoiffeurs themfelves have applauded the

detaiļs

5

details of fine poetry, which are not uncommon
in it.   It has thus appeared to unite the fuffrages
of all; and even its enemies have not had the
courage to examine it rigidly.   The plan of the
work is fo licentious, that they have not undertaken to eftimate the merit of its execution, or
that of the extraneous matter; they have for-
borne to touch it, as pirates avoid a town that
is feeble and defencelefs, but in which they know
the plague rages.   From thefe confiderations
alone, the Pucelle might already be ranked
much beneath the Orlando.

The pleafantries of Ariofto have, in general,
nothing at which modefty can take exception :
if fome few of his tales pafs fomewhat beyond
the boundaries of fimple fport, his language,
and the age in which he lived, concur in his
extenuation.   We admired the exceptionable
parts of Rabelais, when the Italians fmiled at
Joconda.

And this tale, the moft licentious of any in
Ariofto, is not put into the mouth of the poet.
It is a hoftefs who relates it, who tells it to a
lover that has recently experienced a moft cruel
mortification from his miftrefs; this pretty ftory
is fo well adapted to comfort him, and the author paffes on fo rapidly to objects with which
the niceft delicacy cannot be offended, that
criticifm

criticifm is difarmed before fhe has time to be difpleafed.

The other occafions which might excite feverity are rare in the Orlando; whereas in the Pucelle of the eighteenth century, there is fcarcely a canto which has any claim to our indulgence. Modefty is inceffantly hurt, and that in the groffeft degree; even the coloring does not difguife the offenfivenefs of the defign. Scarcely can we excufe the author in having fometimes borrowed the pencil of La Fontaine, and almoft throughout ufed the brufh of Aretin.

By this alone then, as I have faid, this fecond poem, did it poffefs in other refpects every perfection of which this fpecies of literature is capable, could not bear a contraft with the Orlando, which is juftly ranked amongft the moft glorious monuments of Italy. But unfortunately it has not even this merit. The author has evidently fet before him Ariofto as a model, and, notwithftanding, he has in no refpect followed him, he has produced neither an original nor a copy. His poem is a monftrous affemblage of detached pieces collected together, fometimes indeed dazzling from their agreeable fallies, but which no more conftitute a poem than the hundred new novels compofe a romance.

The

The Orlando is itfelf of a nature apparently very extravagant. The Jerufalem, the Æneid, the Iliad, are grave and heroic from end to end. If in the fifth book of the Latin poem you meet with the adventure of the pilot thrown into the fea by the rage of the captain; if Virgil amufes himfelf in defcribing him well foaked, throwing up the falt water he has fwallowed, and the Greeks enjoying his difafter and its confequences; it is in a defcription of Games that this caricature is placed, it occupies but a corner of the picture, which is moreover wholly defigned to exhibit a fcene of feftivity and diverfion. The adventure of eating the tables, and the comic verfe of little Julius,

> Menfas confumere ipfas,

is no pleafantry; it is the ground of a ftory long before admitted among the antiquities of Rome, fince we meet with it again in hiftory, where it is handed down to us in profe.

The Odyffey is widely different from the Iliad, it is even almoft the oppofite extreme. Homer has not painted on the fame canvas the battles of the gods, and the metamorphofes of the companions of Ulyffes; the parting fcene of Andromache, and the lowing of the fkins of the

oxen

oxen which the companions of Ulyffes had eaten a week before.

The Italians were the firft who conceived the idea of intermixing in epic poetry tender events, and ridiculous adventures; of paffing all at once from the moft elevated, to the moft playful ftile; of giving loofe to an imagination to all appearance the moft void of order, without wholly lofing fight of nature; of exhilarating the mind, without ceafing to move the heart; and who have thus thrown into their compofitions all the dignity of tragedy, without excluding from them reprefentations not only taken from common life, but even from fuch fcenes in it as abound with incidents, beft adapted to create mirth. And of all the Italians who have written in this ftile, none have produced any thing worthy of being compared with the Orlando Furiofo. It is the perfeétion of the burlefque, a fpecies of compofition more natural, more refpeétable, and more difficult to attain than is fuppofed; apparently cried down in our language, becaufe it has been too much debafed, but of which our beft authors, with Boileau at their head, have found means to avail themfelves in a great degree, while they were cautious of employing it under its ancient name.

There

There are in it certain limits, which muſt not be left far diſtant, delicate paſſages to be ſeized, light ſhadings which muſt not be too much forced. It is the art with which all theſe regulations are obſerved, that conſtitutes the merit of the Orlando. It is that which Mr. Voltaire propoſed to imitate, what he ſeemed, from his caſt of mind, more capable of imitating than any other, but which unfortunately he has not imitated in the leaſt in his Pucelle.

The ſtile of Arioſto is always adapted to what he has to ſay: in battle it is full of energy, of impetuoſity and grandeur; ſoft, tender, and brilliant in adventures of gallantry, at other times humourous, ſerious, animated or grave, as the ſubject required: whereas, from the beginning to the end of the Pucelle, but one ſtile is diſcoverable. It is a perpetual irony, one continued ſneer throughout.

Arioſto·is maſter of his ſubject, but he makes it his buſineſs; even when jeſting, he has not the air of making game of his heroes or his readers; and this is what Mr. Voltaire does conſtantly. The Italian author is correctly attentive to the cuſtoms of chivalry, but it is with a view to render it reſpectable; the French writer conforms to it likewiſe, but it is to make it ridiculous. The former ſometimes indulges

himſelf

himſelf in humorous tales or laughable adventures, but it is not to his real heroes that they
happen. On the contrary, the latter ſeeks only
to enliven his readers; all is buffoonery and pan-
tomime throughout his poem; the higheſt and
the loweſt of his charácters equally wear this diſ-
graceful badge. Bonneau is truly comic; and it
is one of the beſt drolls in the poem; but Da-
nois, Charles the Seventh, the Pucelle, ſhould
not be ſo, and they notwithſtanding meet with
nothing but ridiculous adventures which degrade
them.

It is in this more eſpecially, in my opinion,
that Mr. Voltaire has miſtaken himſelf. He did
not conſider that there were two ſorts of burleſque; one of which conſiſts in ſpeaking with
dignity, and even force, of things in their nature
trivial and inſignificant; the other in depreciat-
ing ſuch as are really great by vulgar expreſſions
or low ideas. The firſt may pleaſe, and pleaſe
even men of taſte and diſcernment; becauſe there
is nothing in it painful or degrading. What is
beautiful is ſtill beautiful, in ſpite of the inverted
purpoſe to which it is in ſome meaſure applied.
Thus when la Fontaine, in his fable of the Fox
and the Goat, ſays that time, by its continual
progreſs, had eaten into the circular form of the
planet with the ſilver face; this admirable pic-

H ture

ture of the moon in its wane is not spoiled, it becomes more pointed when we find it conclude in the goat's mistaking this star for a half-eaten cheese. This too is the burlesque which pleases in the Lutrin.

It is not so with the other burlesque, that of Scarron, which descends to apply the habits and manners of the lower vulgar to the most dignified characters, to transform the most majestic portraits into despicable caricatures. Clothe a dwarf in the arms of Achilles, let the pigmy under his burthen affect the deportment of the conqueror of Hector, nothing can be more humorous; but should the son of Peleus, in order to counterfeit Thersites, deliberately assume an artificial hump; should the handsomest of men, by way of affording amusement to the spectator, degrade himself so far as to assume the air and mask of the most deformed, will not every one turn with contempt from such a disgusting masquerade? These are the two species of burlesque.

Ariosto is fully sensible of this; he often indulges himself in gaiety, but he no where disparages his work; there is always cast over his pictures, whatever they are, a delicate varnish, which prevents their tarnishing. Mr. Voltaire, on the other hand, in his Pucelle, most plenti-

fully

fully bedaubs his with the coarfeft coloring. The firft canto too, which is written in a pleafing manner, announces quite a different thing from what follows; the reader has not one pleafure which he does not purchafe with pain, not the fatisfaction of one moment, for which he does not experience feveral of indignation and dif-guft.

Befides in the Orlando, comic and burlefque, as in part it is, we difcern a conduct the refult of deliberation, a connected plan; I repeat, that in every canto are to be found leffons and models of magnanimity and decency, together with a variety and inexhauftible profufion of characters, exceeding the exuberance of Homer himfelf in this refpect. Marphifa and Bradaminta are both female warriours, the haughtinefs of the one ferving as a relief to the tender fenfibility of the other. Angelica and Fleurs de Lys are both paffionate lovers, but how finely is the coquetry of the firft depicted! how beautifully is the fidelity of the fecond pourtrayed!

Rolando, Renaud, Roger, Brandimard, Rodomont, Mandricard, Ferragus, &c. are all men of valour, but each recognizable by different features of character and different defcriptions of courage. Rolando and Renaud love with ardor, and fight with generofity. The foul

of

of Roger is more tender, his paſſions leſs violent, but his heart equally noble. Brandimard
is as brave a knight, and as faithful a lover as
either, but friendſhip divides his heart with love,
without weakening its power; Mandricard and
Rodomont are raſh and headſtrong, in whom
tenderneſs aſſumes the ſame fierce and inſulting
charaƈter as their valor; Ferragus, beſides their
defeƈts, is a ſtranger to love, poſſeſſing but the
mere animal part of it.

Add to this diverſity of charaƈter, all that the
heroiſm of chivalry has captivating in it, all
the charms which a prolific imagination is capable of ſupplying; whatever emotions the ten-
dereſt ſenſibility can effeƈt, epiſodes without
number, ſome full of gaiety, as thoſe of Medor
and Angelica, of Doralica and Rodomont;
others pathetic, like thoſe of Zerbin and Iſa-
bella, of Brandimard and Fleur de Lys; and
others again fabulous and amuſing, as the voyage
of Atolphus to the moon: this may ſerve to give
ſome idea of Arioſto's admirable poem. In what
reſpeƈt does the modern Pucelle reſemble it?

Add to this, that in the laſt work, the
ſatire of Mr. Voltaire is carried to the laſt
degree of licentiouſneſs. The editions publiſhed
under the inſpeƈtion of the author, in his old
age, contain a new canto, wholly taken up in

abuſing

abufing his enemies, whom he transforms into galley-flaves, and who being delivered from the oar by their king, teftify their gratitude in no other way than by robbing him. This abufe of talent is atrocious. No poet before Mr. Voltaire ever indulged himfelf in the like ribaldry, and unhappily he has given way to it again, in a manner almoft equally fcandalous, in his poem of the War of Geneva.

Let us conclude this painful article, which a regard to truth forces from me, and agree, in fpite of the commencement of the cantos in the Pucelle, which are moft of them admirable; in fpite of the charming digreffions, which are frequent in this work; and notwithftanding the favorable reception it met with from the public; that the poetical glory of Mr. Voltaire would have fuffered no diminution if he had not given this additional proof of his fecundity. It would even have gained much from its fuppreffion, fince it indicates rather the limitation, than the extent of his genius.

OF

Mr. VOLTAIRE's

TRAGEDIES.

IT is very remarkable, that the firſt and the laſt ſteps of Mr. Voltaire have been towards the theatre: he finiſhed his literary life with Irene, as he began it with Oedipus. This boiſterous and ſplendid career ſeemed, indeed, to offer the ſtrongeſt allurements to a young man fraught with all the enthuſiaſm of youth, and full of that efferveſcence which the view of great models inſpires in a mind ſenſible of their excellence: the ardor of production is then as ſtrong in the moral as in the phyſical ſyſtem in every man whoſe organization is happily formed; and in him that this was not a blind or tranſitory paſſion, which had miſtaken its ſtrength, or the deſtination of its powers, his ſucceſs has ſufficiently ſhewn.

It

It is true, indeed, that in his tragedies we
are not to look for those developements of
the human heart, so juft, so delicate, and so
pathetically interefting, which conftitute the
charm of Racine's pieces; or that force of
genius, and profundity of thought, that chain
of reasoning, and fubtilty of difcrimination, if
I may be allowed the term, which diftinguifh
thofe of Corneille; or even the art of dialogue,
carried by both thofe authors to its height of
perfection; that is to fay, that play of attack
and defence, thofe refources at once natural and
unexpected, which enrich the fcene, and leave
the audience at a lofs whether moft to admire the
propriety or rapidity of the replies.

' Alzira, Merope, and Tancred, are fine tragedies. In the duke de Foix, or rather in the part
of Lifois, the political principles, the magani-
mity, and the heroic delicacy of a gallant knight,
who loves, pities, and follows his monarch, without approving his wanderings, are moft happily
defcribed. Mahomet and Semiramis poffefs their
refpective merits; but, in point of invention,
have they any thing worthy of being fet in competition with the three firft acts of the Horatii;
with this fuperftructure raifed by the genius of
Corneille on a fingle word found in Livy; with
the contraft between a republican youth, whofe
heroifm

heroifm degenerates into barbarity, and a true hero in whom a fpirit of patriotifm is blended with other virtues, with thofe propenfities naturally dear to all tender minds, with thofe fhadings fo fkilfully preferved between the conjugal affection of a wife, the violent paffion of a miftrefs, and the tender but mafculine regard of a father grown old in the perfuafion, that every domeftic tie fhould be facrificed to the duty we owe our country; to this ingenious and probable error, whence refults the falfe conclufion which forces from the old man, that expreffion fo grand, fo fimple, and fo natural in a Roman, while at the fame time fo terrible and fublime, " Let him die."

Thefe three firft acts appear to me to have reached, perhaps to have exceeded the bounds of human capacity; no theatre, in any age, appears to me to have come near them: Corneille himfelf after this effort was never able to raife to the like height; but in paffages where he does not run into the oppofite extreme, he preferves his fuperiority over Mr. Voltaire, in common with every other dramatic writer.

The refignation of Gufman, in Alzira, is doubtlefs a magnificent reprefentation; it is not without reafon thofe lines are celebrated, wherein it is preferved,

" Of our religions, &c."

But

But is not the pardon granted by Auguftus, in Cuma, ftill more fublime? Gufman in reality does no more than obey the dictates of his religion, perhaps he can hardly be allowed the merit of having fulfilled them : about to expire, it is fcarcely poffible for him to behave otherwife. Inftances are not uncommon of men of harfh and even barbarous difpofitions relenting into tendernefs on a death-bed : in fuch moments revenge becomes weak, as it is perceived to be inefficient, and power is difregarded, as it can be no longer enjoyed ; befides how great reafon has the dying Spaniard to accufe himfelf of having injured his rival?

But in the cafe of Auguftus, it was while in perfect health ; when the lives of his enemies were at his abfolute difpofal ; while the power of vengeance was eafy, and the pleafure of enjoying it certain, that he grants a pardon ; and to whom ? to men ftained with ingratitude and treafon ; to a knot of confpirators, whom the blackeft malice and the bafeft treachery had combined together for his deftruction : under fuch circumftances, it is the freedom of agency, the generofity of the facrifice, which conftitutes its grandeur. Ordinary men admire the fentiments of Gufman ; thofe of Auguftus force tears from heroes.

The

The like obfervation will hold good, with regard to the part of Paulina, in Polieuctes : a part unfortunately weakened and even degraded by what furrounds it; and the more worthy of admiration, as, like the three firft acts of the Horatii, it is wholly of the author's own invention, as he could not have gathered a fingle idea on the fubject, either from the ancients or moderns.

Racine himfelf has none of thefe flafhes of genius : but then how ably is he fuftained; how equal throughout; what perfection does he not poffefs, and that in every fpecies! Burrhus, Agrippina, Achmet, prove fufficiently that had he oftener taken other paffions than love for his fubject, he would have arrived, though by a different path, to an equal perfection even with Corneille himfelf, in that particular *forte* for which the latter is diftinguifhed. If the public ftill perfift in the opinion that he was capable of defcribing tendernefs alone, it is one of thofe errors fo common in literature, and which it is impoffible to explain or to reform. Accuftomed to applaud in him that fpecies of merit of which he has given the moft abundant proofs; and which being of itfelf fufficient to eftablifh his claim to genius, it became unneceffary to feek other excellencies in him, and it has therefore been tacitly concluded that he had them not.

9 That

That alone will no more authorize us in placing Mr. Voltaire on an equal footing with him in this respect, than we have already found him entitled to hold with Corneille in the other. Zara is the only piece wherein the latter has attempted to describe the fury of war, and the transports of love. But Zara is wholly borrowed: Orosmanes is no other than the Roxana of Bajazet, metamorphofed into a man. A fevere critic might possibly urge that the original has lost much of its delicacy by the exchange, without having acquired any additional strength; that the adventitious matter, as being the author's own, is still more weakened, and that in spite of its reputation, this is one of the feeblest of his dramatic works; but if from the circumstance alone, that the principal character is but an imitation, it does not confer on Mr. Voltaire the privilege of ranking as a rival of Racine, in those lists wherein the latter has so succefsfully distinguished himself.

And of this he was fully fenfible: this was his fole effort. He did not deceive himself, and the proof that he did not, rests equally in his theatrical as in his other productions; possessed of every imaginable mental resource, he was deficient in that eloquence of the heart, those powers of expression, sometimes soft and at others

others impetuous, at once abundant and chaste, which are neceſſary to an adequate delineation of the conflicts, the delicacies, and the tranſports of love; an eloquence, preciſion, and abundance, which in poetry has been granted among the Romans to Virgil alone, among the Italians to Arioſto and Taſſo, in France to the author of Phædra, and among other nations to no one.

Mr. Voltaire, like Corneille, has contented himſelf with making this paſſion a ſecondary aid, which ſerves only to extend his pieces to their proper length. In Semiramis, Mahomet, and Cataline, it has no other office. It is not love by which the ſpectator feels himſelf affected in Tancred; but the generoſity and magnanimity which dazzles throughout the piece. In the Orphan of China, the barbarous paſſion of Gengiſkan has none of the characteriſtics which render love tragical; on the contrary, it borders, as well from its nature as expreſſion, on the oppoſite deſcription.

Mr. Voltaire, while he juſtly obſerved the error of Corneille, who enfeebled his pieces by introducing a paſſion which, when it does not excite the ſole intereſt, diminiſhes its force, has nevertheleſs imitated him. It is a tribute he pays to cuſtom, to convenience, to the conſtitution, as we may ſay, of the theatre, whence it

is

is not allowable wholly to exclude women; and where it would be often very difficult to find them employment, were they not engaged either in making, or in receiving declarations of love.

Nor are we to expect in Mr. Voltaire's pieces, that conduct, that art of arranging, opening, and thickening a plot, that skill in the management of his scenes, in adding to the embarrassment, and increasing the interest of the piece, of never leaving the stage empty, or occupied by characters brought on for the sole purpose of filling it; an art which was perfectly understood by Racine alone; who does not even possess it himself in all his pieces.

Lastly, We are not to require from Mr. Voltaire that delicacy, purity, and harmony, that noble simplicity, elegant, but not oftentatious, that poetry of sentiment rather than of style, which expresses with equal simplicity and richness, and always in the justest terms, without the restraint of rhyme or measure detracting in the least from the propriety of language, the ragings of love, the fury of ambition, or the subtilties of policy; excellencies, which, in our language, and I believe in every other, were granted to one man alone, and that always the same, to the inimitable Racine, who died at so early a period, so soon torn from his country,

by

by whom he was very moderately honored in his life time, fordidly repaid, by the court for the fervices he had rendered the language and poetry in general, punifhed for an honeft and praife-worthy action by a difgrace which coft him his life; and laftly, even at the prefent day, held in light eftimation by his own countrymen; who, had he been born in England, Italy, or Germany, would have had ftatues erected to him in his life, and temples at his death.

The perfection of his language is fo great, that half its excellence is loft in reprefentation. His pieces are highly finifhed and exquifite pictures, which, to difcover their full excellence, require to be infpected at leifure and with reflection.

The fhades too of his bewitching poetry are fo delicate, that it is difficult to find actors capable of conceiving and expreffing them. Madam de Sevigné has been harfhly reproached for the decree fhe may be faid to have pronounced on the merits of the two authors who divided the theatre in her time; and in the preference fhe gave to Corneille, by her comparifon of Racine to a modifh tafte, to coffee, which as fhe faid would not maintain its ground.

Madam de Sevigné, even in this error, feems to me to have given a proof of her judgment. She expreffed very happily the fentiments which
a diffipated

a diffipated woman, who had lived a good deal
in the world, and whofe opinion of dramatic
productions arofe rather from reprefentation than
reading, was likely to form; one who was determined in her choice by the emotion fhe felt at
the former, and who carried with her into the
clofet the impreffions fhe felt at the theatre.
Doubtlefs the terrible graces of Corneille, the
Michael Angelo of poetry, muft affect both her
and all of her age, in a more lively degree,
than the foft, eafy, and natural, though learned
tints of Racine, who may be deemed the
Raphael of that art. There is fcarcely any
company by which the characters of the Horatii,
Cinna, Polieuctes, &c. are not tolerably performed. But where are we to find actors who
are capable of declaiming, without monotony,
Hippolitus's declaration of love, the tender remonftrances of Iphigene in the part of Phædra,
to vary the tones as the different paffions require,
in that of Roxana, to hit the precife degree,
fometimes of confidence, at others of rage;
fometimes of the pathetic, and at others of
rancour, which are neceffary to it; to reconcile
in the character of Achilles the anger of the fon
of Peleus, with the dignity and grandeur which
Racine has preferved to him amidft his tranfports.

He himfelf inftructed the celebrated Champ-
meflé. The manner in which fhe played his
characters

characters made her pafs for the beft actrefs
of her age. It was thought fhe added to the
beauties of her author; but on the contrary,
all her merit confifted in availing herfelf of his
inftructions, that fhe might not lofe any of them.
Accordingly Mad. Sevigné again fays, that to
difcern the beauties of the tragedy of Bajazet,
we ought to fee the actrefs. She formed her judgment in this alfo like a fenfible woman, who
read little, but judged well of what fhe faw.
Her only fault was that of forming too hafty a
decifion; of not allowing herfelf time to examine
whether fhe would not have found in reading
Bajazet what fhe had fo much admired in the
reprefentation; and had fhe done fo, fhe would
have found much more. But fhe had not the
neceffary leifure to be correct; and in more
ferious affairs, there are fo few men who take
this neceffary time, that in a point of literature
we may well excufe the want of it in a woman.

However this may be, it does not appear that
Mr. Voltaire in this refpect can be confidered
as poffeffing any fuperior merit to diftinguifh
him from his predeceffors: though infinitely
fuperior to Corneille, not in fome particular
paffages, wherein Corneille has not even an equal;
but in his general tafte, in point of correctnefs
and elegance of ftyle; much is ftill wanting in

I   all

all thefe particulars, before he will be thought to excel, or even to equal Racine.

The proper word is never wanting in Racine. In Mr. Voltaire's poetry it is feldom found. We difcover even that he has not been at the pains to feek it. Thus in the Death of Cæfar we find,

> " Cæfar was a hero, but Cæfar was a *traitor.*"

Traitre moft affuredly is only placed there, becaufe the verfe that precedes it ends in *maitre.* The proper word would have been tyrant, or ufurper, &c. never was the brave, the generous Cæfar accufed of treafon or perfidy.

We find the fame word equally mifapplied in Merope. Polifontes fays of Egiftus,

> " It is your fon, madam, or 'tis a *traitor.*"

He fhould have faid an impoftor. Egiftus, in giving himfelf even falfely for the Queen's fon, is an impoftor, and not a traitor.

We read in Semiramis,

> " And unpropitious heaven
> Hath *corrupted* the courfe of his profperity."

Is *corrupted* the proper word ? Racine fays of Athalia,

> " Of late a fpectre moft importunate
> Hath interrupted the courfe of my profperity."

In

In Œdipus, Philoctetes, speaking of Hercules, says,

> " From waiting at the altars
> And raising tombs to that great hero,
> I come ——————"

Why tombs ? Altars may be raised in honor of a deity, becaufe many in reality may be confecrated to him. But the fame man can have but one tomb.

In Zara, Lufignan, in order to exprefs the refurrection of Jefus Chrift, and defcribe the holy fepulchre, fays :

> " Behold the fpot, whence he drew life
> From out the filent grave."

Would Racine have expreffed himfelf thus ? Is life to be found in the grave ? The author of Andromache finely fays,

> " Thou feek'ft her with thine eyes ;
> Thou fpeak'ft to her with thine heart."

He has faid,

> " Full plainly haft thou heard thofe fighs
> Which fear'd to be repell'd."

But what a difference between them, between thefe flights, which animate and perfonify every thing ; which excite no other furprife in the reader, than that which fuch energy of thought united with fuch eafe muft neceffarily produce, and the languid turn of the King of Cyprus !

In Tancred, Orbaffan fays to Argira :

> " The tie which now unites us once again
> Had ne'er ta'en place, but that in angry ftrife,
> Now buried in oblivion, my fond heart
> Which hated, ftill efteem'd you."

Hated, perhaps, is the proper word, but what a
fhocking harfhnefs !

Racine allowed himfelf to fay,

> " Did you e'en hate me, I could not complain."

There is no ear but muft perceive, that in the
laft verfe, the word has all the foftnefs it is
capable of, and that in the other inftance, its
natural harfhnefs is greatly augmented.

Inftances of this kind are innumerable.

In point of elegance, Mr. Voltaire is ftill lefs
qualified to maintain the comparifon.   It is true
he has nearly approached Racine in feveral paffages of Mariamne, Brutus, Semiramis, and
Tancred, and above all in the part of Lifois
Duke de Foix, a part written with a continuation
of grandeur, precifion, force, and fimplicity,
which is truly remarkable.   But in general, he
has rarely piqued himfelf on devoting the neceffary labour, to infure to his poetical works, and
more efpecially to his tragedies, this fpecies of
merit.

Let the two poets be clofely compared, particularly where they have the fame things to
fay,

say ; for inftance, in the reflections of Zara and
Eriphiles, on their mutual ignorance of their
origin.

The daughter of Lufignan thus expreffes herfelf,

   " ————Ha ! What fay'ft thou ? Why
Would'ft thou recal my forrows, Fatima,
Alas, I know not who or what I am,
Not e'en who gave me birth."

Hear the rival of Iphigene :

   " Expos'd for ever to fome new diftrefs,
In earlieft youth to ftrangers' care entrufted ;
E'en from my birth till now, I've liv'd
Unconfcious of a tender mother's fmile,
Or father's kind regard."

The former verfes are not even tolerable profe,
the others are poetical, elegant, and abounding
with pathetic imagery.

Gengifkan and Hippolitus have each to exprefs
a barbarous love ; both are equally at a lofs how
to exprefs a paffion with which they are alike
unacquainted ; but the Tartar has not one expreffion which goes to the heart, or comes from
it, not one that is poetical or affecting, it is a
grofs paffion, grofsly and profaically expreffed :

   " Beware how thou infult'ft excefs of weaknefs,
Which rage already turns to my reproach ;
E'en this avowal may create you danger ;
Dread then my love, and tremble at my favors,

I 3

My

My foul is but too eager for revenge;
And I fhall punifh you for having lov'd you,
Oh pardon me—E'en now amidft my threats I figh;
Quell then this rage, beginning to fubfide,
And by a fingle word decide my empire's fate;
But this important word you muft pronounce.
Say then, without delay, referve, or art,
If you will have my hatred or my love."

What a cold declamation, when contrafted with
that well known paffage of Phædra, fo often
quoted, and fo continually new to every reader
poffeffed of tafte and fentiment.

"Behold before you an unhappy prince,
A ftriking monument of frantic pride;
Who long a rebel to all pow'rful love,
Have oft infulted his poor captive's chains;
Pitying the fate of thofe whofe wrecks I faw,
I deem'd myfelf fecure: and from the fhore
Thought to behold unhurt the ftorm around me,
Now made fubfervient to the common lot,
What wond'rous pow'r tranfports me from myfelf,
Which in a moment humbles my rafh pride,
And proves this haughty foul is now enflaved.
In all the agonies of grief and fhame,
For fix long months I've borne the fatal dart
By which I'm pierc'd: againft myfelf and you
I vent my fruitlefs vows. I fly you, prefent,
Abfent, your lov'd, adored image haunts me—
I trace it in the foreft's gloom, the day's bright beam,
The fhade of night; each objeĉt I behold
Refleĉts thofe charms, I ftrive in vain to fly from;
And ferves alike, fpite of myfelf, to give you up

The

The rebel flave Hippolytus. E'en now
In vain I ftrive to feek my former felf;
My bow, my car, my jav'lin ufelefs lie;
Great Neptune's leffons are forgotten;
My fteeds no longer hear their mafter's voice,
While every grove re-echoes with my groans.
A conqueft fo unworthy makes you blufh——
How fierce the heart your beauty has fubdued!
How ftrange a captive in fo fweet a toil!
The offer therefore fhould the more be priz'd;
I fpeak a language I am little vers'd in;
Let not my vows be deem'd the lefs fincere,
Becaufe perhaps they're ill exprefs'd; vows which
Hippolytus could form for you alone."

Doubtlefs Gengifkan, at a mature age, poffeffed of uncontrouled power and enraged, in addreffing a woman whom he wifhes to force from her hufband, ought not to ufe the fame fubmiffive language, the like foft and infinuating eloquence in which the young and fufceptible Hippolytus addreffes his miftrefs, young, fufceptible, and independent like himfelf; but he ought equally to aim at enlivening what he has to fay by imagery; he fhould equally endeavour to unite energy with elegance, and to avoid thofe turns of expreffion defective in themfelves, and contrary to the fpirit of the language; fuch as,

" I fhall punifh you, for having lov'd you."

Or weak ones, fuch as,

" E'en this avowal."

Or

Or idle and embarrassed, as,

> ——————————" excefs of weaknefs,
> Which rage already turns to my reproach."

Is an example equally ftriking, of the aftonifhing fuperiority of Racine ftill wanting? Let us attend to the fentiments of Gengifkan and Achmet on the fame fubject, that of tendernefs and policy; who concur in preferring ambition and their perfonal fecurity, to the delights which fuccefsful love is capable of conferring.   Behold Achmet,

> " ————And doft thou wifh me at my years
> To ferve a vile apprenticefhip to love?
> And that a heart which toil and age have harden'd,
> Should follow pleafure's vain, imprudent dictates?
> Far other charms are thofe by which I'm caught:
> I love in her the blood from which fhe's fprung;
> To her united, and to Bajazet,
> He fees me raife a barrier 'gainft himfelf;
> A Vizier ever muft alarm his Sultan.
> No fooner nam'd, than dreaded and fufpected;
> Lur'd by the plenteous fpoil of his deftruction,
> And prompted by capricious cruelty,
> His mafter feldom lets him fee old age.
> Bajazet now much loves and honors me,
> His daily perils ferve to wake regard;
> Once firmly feated on the throne, perhaps,
> He'll view in me a ufelefs friend or flave;
> Should this be fo, and he demand my head,
> Regardlefs of my loyalty or love,
> Ofmin, I will not fay—but I prefume
> It may be long ere his command's obey'd.

I'll

I'll ſerve the Emp'ror with fidelity,
But leave to vulgar minds to worſhip tyrants—
The mad extravagance to bleſs the arm
That's rais'd to ſhed my blood is not for me."

What ſays Gengiſkan?

" Since here my ſoul firſt own'd a conqu'ror,
Since firſt my haughty ſpirit was ſubdued,
My heart e'er ſince retain'd its former freedom,
Safe from the power of degrading love.
Idamia, I confeſs, rais'd in my reſtleſs mind
Emotions ſtrange, and pangs till then unknown.
Our northern caves and barren plains, produce
No beauty that can faſcinate the ſenſes;
The fierce companions of our hardy labors,
Partake our ſpoils and emulate our courage:
In theſe mild climes, from ſoft Idamia's eyes,
From her whoſe ev'ry word and geſture charms,
I drank a new and ſubtle poiſon.——
Thanks to the cruelty that rais'd my anger,
Contempt diſpell'd this dang'rous charm;
The ſov'reign, but myſterious paſſion of the ſoul,
My happineſs, had caus'd my utter ruin.
Freed by her coldneſs, I purſu'd my bold
Career, and purchas'd boundleſs victory
For weak, unmanly ſighs.   Th' unworthy flame
With which I burnt, no more ſhall fire my heart;
Without a pang I baniſh the baſe thought,
Woman ſhall ne'er poſſeſs ſuch influence o'er me;
I will forget her, and at leiſure leave her
To feel my ſcorn, and curſe her rebel pride.
Octar, I charge you, name her not."

The

The object of all these quotations, is by no means to detract from the merit of Mr. Voltaire, but merely to evince the superiority of Racine over him, in that species of merit which has hitherto come under our consideration.

What characterises the former, what is in an especial manner a merit of his own, what, in my opinion, entitles him to the claim of originality as an author, as the founder of a new drama, and the creator of an original manner, is the variety, the multiplicity of portraits, with which his pieces abound. On this head, he has the advantage over both Racine and Corneille.

The idea conceived of the variety of the latter is perhaps no more founded in justice, than the reproach of sameness repeated against the former. It is in reality Corneille who may be justly accused of too much uniformity.—In his pieces the names alone are varied; the characters and passions are the same: the sentiments are alike in all. Haughtiness, pretended Roman magnanimity, sometimes swelled to a gigantic size, are constantly the prevailing features, a desire of revenge, oftentimes atrocious, and frequently expressed with an inconceivable mixture of turgidness and familiarity. Of six or seven pieces which are in representation, this is the ground of four; the Cid, Cinna, Rodogune, and the

Death

Death of Pompey. Chimena, Emilia, Cornelia, all demand the punifhment of a father, or a hufband, and the abominable Cleopatra, in Rodogune, enumerates revenge among her pretexts for the horrors fhe meditates.

Racine would probably have diverfified his Theatre much more, had he not renounced the exercife of his genius when it had attained its full vigor. Britannicus, Iphigenia, Bajazet, Phædra, Athalia, have no common fimilitude to each other, but this great man becoming indolent at too early a period, has done fo little, that, if we may fo exprefs it, he feems barren in the midft of fecundity. He has delineated but few paffions, becaufe he has written but few pieces; and if he had not produced Bajazet and Athalia, it would probably have been faid, that he was incapable of fucceeding, but in fubjects on which he borrowed his ideas from the ancients.

Mr. Voltaire chalked out for himfelf a wider circle. He has, as we may fay, brought mankind at large upon his theatre. He has, under various forms, introduced on it every intereft and paffion which actuate the human heart. To thefe he has added fometimes ftriking defcriptions of foreign manners, and obfolete cuftoms; at others, under national names, he has alluded no lefs happily to our own habits; a

fpecies

species of writing which he may even be accused of not having carried so far as he might have done, and which has degenerated in the hands of his feeble imitators.

In Alzira, the customs of America are opposed to those of Europe; in the Orphan of China, the virtues of a civilized people are contrasted with the violences of a barbarous one: in Tancred is displayed all the pomp, the grandeur, and sublime magnanimity of chivalry, such at least as it is described in romances: maternal tenderness shines in Merope: the foundation of Mahometanism is pourtrayed in Mahomet, with vigor, if not with fidelity: the intrigues of courts, the hidden crimes, and secret remorse, which poison and degrade external pomp, are exposed to view in Semiramis. Even in those pieces of which the general character is less perfect, there are, notwithstanding, some characters of great excellence to be found, and all of a different description of beauty; such is that which I have before remarked, of Lisois, in the Duke de Foix; of Electra, in Orestes; Cicero, in Rome Preserved; of Fulvia, in the Triumvirate, and of Athamara, in the Scythians, &c.

This abundance, enriched by variety, is doubtless a valuable excellence, but in my opinion,

Mr.

Mr. Voltaire poffeffes two others, ftill more precious and eftimable, which are no lefs exclufively his own, and for one of which I have not perceived that any one has hitherto given him credit.

The firft confifts in that philofophy, at the fame time dignified and pathetic, with which his good pieces abound. The other is that of not having admitted into them any villainous, bafe, or abfolutely deteftable character; of not having racked his imagination to conceive, and to find language and employment for fuch characters as Narciffus, Mathan, and ftill lefs for a Cleopatra, Rodogune, Maximin, Felix, and others of this defcription, oftentatioufly difplayed by one of his rivals, fometimes efcaping the other, and multiplied to the moft fcandalous degree on the modern ftage, which thence affumes rather the appearance of a field devoted to villainy, than a fchool of virtue.

This is a point on which I prefume to think almoft all our authors have been miftaken, who have difplayed their talents in this fpecies of compofition. It is neceffary, fay they, to avail ourfelves of the feelings of the audience; but at the fame time they have forgotten that there fhould be a proportion between the fhock, and the organs which are to fuftain it.

In

In common life, in fpite of our invincible propenfity to intereft ourfelves in favor of every being who feems to fuffer, if his cries are continual, if they degenerate into fcreams, if his wounds are hideous and openly difplayed, we are prefently impreffed with horror, rather than pity. We fly from a fpectacle which operates as a punifhment, and become indifferent from excefs of fenfibility : it is the ftring of the violin which lofes its fweetnefs from being too much ftretched.

This principle is univerfally true, equally on the theatre as elfewhere. There the organs fhould not be wounded, from a too great defire of affecting them ; which muft happen, even in comedy, when the humour is too grofs, or the vices too odious ; and in tragedy, when the misfortunes, and for a ftronger reafon, when the guilt of the heroes is extended to a degree of atrocioufnefs.

Has not Moliere fomewhat violated this fitnefs in his Tartuffe ? This piece poffeffes fome moft excellent ftrokes of humor, and fome mafterly traits of character : but the outlines of the picture appear to me neither juft nor pleafing : his impoftor is at the fame time too bafe, too knavifh, and too grofs ; the real Tartuffes would be much lefs to be dreaded, if they were not more

ſkilful :

fkilful: thofe among them who are capable of equal guilt, ufe very different means to conceal it.

Further, an abufe of religion, pufhed to fuch an excefs, becomes more properly an object of juftice than comedy. We do not laugh at a fcene of horror; and the character of the Tartuffe is fo criminal, that the poet had no way left of difpofing of him but by fending him to prifon, by an immediate and irregular act of power, by a lettre de cachet, which affuredly is neither inftructive nor humorous.

The rule is the fame, and even ftill more effential to tragedy. Its object is to imprefs and affect the heart: true, but in order that the tears may be gentle, it muft be gentle fenfations that produce them, not painful ones, which force them from us.

Even in cataftrophes, which the audience has forefeen, thofe which they appear to have fought, but, in order to partake as it were, in the horror attending them, fuch as public executions, (thefe, as we know, are tragedies of the vulgar) in thofe fcenes of terror to which the fpectators are attracted by the hope and the expectation of being affected, the fentiment muft proceed from one of thefe two fources; either the guilt is of fuch a nature as abfolutely to extinguifh all compaffion, in which cafe the fufferings of the victims

3   excite

excite no pity, or their remorſe, when compared with their crimes, obtain their pardon; the audience then becomes intereſted in their ſate, and every ſpectator awaits the fatal moment with painful anxiety.

Both reaſon and experience then ſeem to concur, in admoniſhing the poet not to carry theatrical emotion to that exceſs by which it becomes annihilated, or changed into fixed grief; which, I repeat, can never fail to happen, when the characters are too criminal, or too unfortunate.

But how happens it, that a principle thus evident ſhould have been unknown, even to the moſt celebrated adepts at that epocha, when the art received its greateſt perfection? Whence is it, that in ſpite of the concurring reflections of the greateſt geniuſes, in a long ſeries of ages, the axiom has prevailed, that the object of tragedy ſhould be to give a rude ſhock to the paſſions, and not to make the feelings of an audience gently vibrate? How happens it, as a conſequence, that while nature and good ſenſe direct us to remove from the ſcene whatever has a tendency to wound the heart, with at leaſt as much care as we do that which may offend the eye or the ear, the ſtage has been crouded with hideous ſpectacles, which would make an audience of executioners ſhudder? How comes it that they have been not

only

only attempted, but applauded? The folution of this ftrange problem will perhaps be eafily found, by recurring to the infancy of our drama, and tracing its origin and progrefs. Although this digreffion may become fomewhat long, I hope I fhall be excufed in making it. It is not foreign to an Art which engaged the attention of him who is the fubject of this work for near a century, and it may contribute to introduce a reformation which to me feems really important, as far as a reformation of this nature can be.

It is to Greece we are indebted for the drama, in common with all the other arts. In architecture, fculpture, poetry, and eloquence, this ingenious people foon emerged from barbarifm. The theatre alone retained among them in its maturity, the fame character it had in its origin, and unhappily for us, this was a monftrous one.

Whatever might have been the unknown caufe, which directed the tafte of the inventors of the dramatic art, and thence formed that of the audience, certain it is, that they appear to have adopted from choice, the moft horrible fubjects: crimes often as difficult to be conceived, as committed; and what is very ftrange, perpetrated often by virtuous perfons, whofe guilt is rather to be attributed to the rigour of their fate, than to the depravity of their principles. Such,

K   for

for inftance, are thofe of Oreftes, Phædra [1], and above all Œdipus. Œdipus the moft fcandalous of all fubjects, which conveys no inftruction, except, that with the moft fpotlefs minds, men are often doomed to perpetrate the moft horrid guilt, and that by the eternal decrees of Providence, the punifhment due only to atrocious villainy, fometimes falls on the head of the virtuous and innocent: a terrible and defponding moral, impious in its tendency, and from which it is impoffible that any one good effect fhould refult.

Œdipus, a good hufband, a good father, and a good king, excites indignation and murmur, rather than pity, when we fee him not only involuntarily become guilty of parricide and inceft, but punifhed with rigour by the gods, for thofe offences which themfelves have caufed him to commit, and to which he was no way confcious.

Doubtlefs, from daily obfervation, a reflecting man may be held excufed, in admitting a predeftination, a fupernatural power, which, in fpite of ourfelves, difpofes the events on which our fate depends. It is but too evident that there are fome perfons born under the influence of a

---

[1] Phædra is virtuous, fince the immediate interference of the Divinity was neceffary to corrupt her. Oreftes has even received orders from the Gods to avenge his father.

malignant

malignant fortune, which they cannot elude, while others appear to inherit from nature a propenfity to evil which they are unable to refift. The former, notwithftanding the integrity of their principles, are all their life the fport of, and often fall victims to, the rigors of fociety; detraction even follows them to the grave, and after death forbids them the reparation due to fuffering virtue. The latter, feem in an efpecial manner .devoted to villainy from their organization, and the fatisfaction with which they commit it, and thefe again do not always meet with the punifhment they deferve— but can more be granted to fate?

At leaft in this fyftem which confiders the Deity as a capricious and fantaftic workman, guided, in the diftribution of human propenfities, and the deftiny of mankind, by mere whim; the honeft man, abandoned to perfecution, retains his fentiments of virtue and innocence to confole him under his misfortunes; and a *Cartouche* impelled to perverfe actions, has received, together with the vocation to evil, that difpofition which caufes him to love it: the one is unhappy, but irreproachable: the other contributes, at leaft in a fecondary degree, to thofe crimes with which he is ftained : Providence has deftined him to live and die a villain; be it fo: but with the lot of a villain he has apportioned him the mind of one—and this fyftem again is very fevere.

But the hiftory of Œdipus fuppofes one ftill more terrible: this Prince abhors vice, and muft notwithftanding commit it: his mind is unfpotted, while his hand is embrued in blood! And, after committing crimes to which he has not confented, he is punifhed by the Deity, becaufe he has yielded, not to an impulfe of depravity, but to an irrefiftible fate, originally allotted to him : once again, this fyftem infpires one with horror. Such a difpenfation makes of the Divinity a monfter, a hundred times more wicked than thofe frail beings whom he dooms to wretchednefs with fuch wanton cruelty.

Is it not enough that Providence fhould have given men that terrible power of treating innocence like guilt? At leaft, our religion abfolves it of injuftice, by confidering this world as a ftate of paffage, as a feafon of trial, the defects of which have no influence on futurity. It places beyond life an Almighty Revifor, a Judge of Judges, who reverfes thefe dreadful decrees; a Judge, who in his turn punifhes the authors of injuftice, and delivers the victims of it. But the Greeks had not this refource. They did not place Œdipus in the Elyfian fields. He, notwithftanding his integrity, was not only guilty, but punifhed, for crimes which the Gods had ordained him to commit: he feems to have exifted, but to afford

a terrible

a terrible monument of their defpotifm and in-juftice.

I repeat it, were this horrid fyftem a true one, is it one of thofe which a reflecting government fhould endeavour to render common, and proclaim with a loud voice on the ftage?

With this ftrange fyftem of metaphyfics, the Greeks united manners which even the difference of times and tafte cannot excufe. In Sophocles, Oreftes ftabs his mother in cool blood: we hear her wretched fcreams, and her daughter Electra, who is alone on the ftage, applauds the parricide, and encourages her brother in the perpetration of it.

In Alceftes alfo, which with fo abfurd a plot, poffeffes fuch pathetic details, Admetes loads his aged father with revilings, in him more criminal than all the enormities of Œdipus, becaufe they are the refult of will and of reflection: the fubject of his anger, is the refufal which the good old man pleafantly makes of dying for him. I know not if in literature a greater abfurdity was ever hazarded, than the reafoning of P. Brumoy, in juftification of this fhocking indecency. " It " offends us only," fays he, " from the alteration " which has taken place in our manners: the " Greeks would have been equally hurt at thofe, " fince eftablifhed in other countries." In fupport of this, the learned Jefuit cites the fury of fingle combat, fo long retained in Europe, and the cuftom of the Iroquois, who put their fathers to death when they become old : but this comparifon itfelf condemns the Grecian manners : Can it be deemed a juftification of them, to compare them with fuch as authorize affaffinations and parricides ?

Befides, a father murdered by his fon, or a fon murdered by his father, has been prefented on no ftage. When duels have been hazarded, as in the Cid, what is blameworthy or offenfive in the action, is compenfated for by the grandeur which accompanies it, or by the beauties which it produces ; but what is the refult of the tragical farces on which we are now treating, and what would it be if we had all the tragedies as prodigioufly multiplied on the Athenian theatre as on our own !

Do not thefe manners prove, that if the Greeks, as inventors, were worthy of being looked up to as guides by thofe who were willing to tread in their footfteps, that they were not equally entitled in all refpects to be regarded as models for imitation ? From them were to be acquired the principles of the art which fhould have been applied to wifer and more noble ends. The firft fculptors ufed only wood and ftone : but the Olympian

Jupiter,

Jupiter, and Athenian Minerva, were carved in ivory and gold. Phidias, who brought the art to its perfection, made choice of materials worthy of his skill.

This reformation, the Romans, who were the imitators, and even copyists of the Greeks, in almost every liberal art, failed of making: at least we may presume so, from the declamations of Seneca which we have, and the idea preserved to us of what the tragedies of Ovid and Varus were, which we have not. The misfortunes of the empire which followed, the ravages of the barbarians, and lastly, in the latter ages, the quarrels between the altar and throne, stifled the dramatic, in common with every other art. The people oppressed with their own misfortunes, but too well realized; had little inducement to repair together to mourn over fictitious woes. Had any poet attempted to draw tears by depicting some striking catastrophe, there was then hardly any family but could have furnished him with a subject.

The modern Italians in the 16th century, cultivated epic poetry with success, which had degenerated since the time of Virgil, but they made but vain and feeble efforts to awaken the tragic muse. Italy was then overrun with wandering Greeks, who, in order to gain a sub-

subsistence,

fiftence, highly extolled the ancient models of their country: they printed Sophocles, Euripides, &c. they reftored them, commented, and tranflated them, but they taught no one the art of imitating them. Their anceftors were unable to do it when they governed the world by their arms: their defcendants did not even conceive an idea of it, when they ruled it only by opinion.

The Spaniards, who were long unknown to the Greeks, and ftill longer the flaves of the Romans, had opened to themfelves an interefting field. This ftrange Melpomene was as new in her nature as that of the Greeks in the days of Thefpis, and was totally independent of her, except in the fingular difparity of uniting Graciofo's buffoons with defpairing lovers; of introducing on the fame fcene a Jodelet and an Achilles.

Ordinary fubjects, ufually taken from common life, but with complicated intrigues, fantaftic incidents, miftakes, favored by the ufe of veils, or (mantas,) in the women, and clokes, or (capas,) in the men; no crimes, no violences, except fuch as a falfe fpirit of bravery and of do neftic delicacy could give rife to, a mixture of defpotifm and gallantry towards the fair fex; which made the men the flaves of their miftreffes,

and

and the tyrants of their fifters; amours croffed, but always happy in the end: in fhort, aftonifh-ing fallies of genius, amidft a barbarifm no lefs ftriking: fuch are the characteriftics of the dramas of the Lopez de Vaga, the Calderonas, the Moretos, &c. too little known, and too much defpifed, but more comic, and a hundred times more worthy of admiration than is ima-gined [2].

At

---

[2] About twenty years ago, on my return from Spain, familiarized with the language, and retaining a lively im-preffion of what I had feen, I ventured to tranflate fome of their pieces. But I muft own, the copies conveyed a very inadequate idea of their originals. I was at that time under the influence of certain principles which fome modern tranf-lators have endeavoured to eftablifh; fuch, for inftance, as that it is the duty of a tranflator to accommodate his verfion to the tafte of his reader, and to amend the text where it is deficient in this refpect.

It is owing to the prevalence of this and fuch like maxims, that the tranflations of the Englifh theatre, and of other literary works, are rendered very ufelefs performances, be-caufe they are faithlefs ones. My Spanifh drama is in a fimilar predicament. It may ferve to afford fome idea of the artifice and conduct of the pieces, of the difpofition and even the tafte of their fcenes; but none of the ftyle of their authors, and the nature of their dramatic poetry. I have frenchified, and confequently fpoiled it, in which I was much to blame. More mature reflection has fince led me to concur with Mr. Voltaire in the opinion, notwithftanding

what

At the revival, or more properly at the birth of letters in France, in the beginning of the 17th century, for the reign of Francis the 1ft. introduced there but a mafquerade of bacchanals, difguifed as mufes; at this epocha, the honor of which is afcribed to Cardinal Richlieu, who, to mention it by the bye, in no way contributed to it, our firft authors, without any referve, made the Spanifh drama their model: they made it the common and only fource whence they drew all their fubjeats.

Some fingular circumftances had caufed that language and literature to become prevalent in France: the courtiers who furrounded the throne,

what may be urged to the contrary, that a tranflation, in order to be inftruaive and ufeful, fhould be literal.

But, owing to the difference of tafte and idiom, it will be ridiculous! Well, it will ferve to render the contraft ftill more ftriking! In order to bring the Europeans acquainted with the drefs and converfation of the Turks, Indians, or Chinefe, would it be an apt expedient to muffle them in our fhort frocks, affign them our viands and liquors, and make them exprefs themfelves in the polifhed periods of Racine or Addifon?

But no body will read tranflations thus literally rendered! Be it fo: in that cafe none will imagine they know the original, but thofe capable of reading the text; there will be no more tranflations, or at leaft there will be no more falfe conclufions drawn from tranflations: and this muft certainly be deemed a benefit to literature.

the

the *petits maitres* in private circles, were Spaniards: as were the heroes both of the dramas and of romance. Corneille, the great Corneille, himfelf began, by affuming the Spanifh cape and the Golila.

But the fcholar foon left his tutors behind him. Having given the Cid after their manner, by the force of his own genius, he produced the Horatii; a piece, by which, as I before obferved, he placed a barrier between himfelf and other dramatic writers, which no one has yet been able to furmount; a piece in which there is nothing but what is really noble; where the guilt which attends the affaffination of Camilla, a fact juftified moreover by hiftory, does not degrade the murderer; nor the weaknefs of the two laft acts derogate from decency, or good manners; where the father of the guilty party, become his advocate, is lefs folicitous to juftify him, than to obtain his pardon in favor of the triumph which preceded the crime. Had Corneille continued to labour in the fame road, he would in every fenfe have been the creator of a new theatre, and the reformer of the old.

Hitherto he owed nothing to the Greeks; he had borrowed nothing from them; perhaps they were wholly unknown to him: but at this period, whether he had lately thought proper to read them,

them, and imagined he ought to follow examples, he who had so lately afforded an inimitable one himself, or whether, (which is more probable) he felt oppressed and disconcerted by the pedantry of the times, which became the resource of such of his rivals, to whom genius was wanting; a pedantry of which he was the victim, from the whole phalanx of criticism being united together against him, from hearing Aristotle spoken of, the Φόβω, κ) ἐλεω, ill explained, and still worse understood, he conceived that in future he ought to treat his subjects after the Grecian mode; to place on the scene vile or furious characters, and accompany sentiments capable of dignifying human nature, with puerilities or horrors calculated only to degrade it; he produced Cinna, Polieuctes, Rodogune, &c. Dramas looked on as *chefs d'œuvres*, and in reality sparkling with admirable beauties.

But he made Emilia a direct fury, who joins perverseness to ingratitude; who openly declares that " Favors flowing from a hated hand operate as injuries; and notwithstanding, does not hesitate to accept them, in order to employ them in seducing the friends of her abused benefactor, who heaps them on her; who declares in express terms, that she would marry Augustus, to have

the

the pleafure of murdering him in his bed [3], &c. He makes Cinna a bafe and deliberate villain, who having from weaknefs confpired againft his prince, his protector, and his friend, under the pretext that he has ufurped the empire of Rome; and obferving him about to make a voluntary refignation of it, preffes him on his knees to retain it in his poffeffion, that he may never want an excufe to affaffinate him; and of this policy he makes no fcruple openly to boaft.

He makes of Felix, in Polieuctes, the bafeft and moft worthlefs villain that ever exifted, an old father, who having married his daughter to a worthy but indigent country gentleman, fome years afterwards, on the return of one of her former lovers, who had acquired a fortune, deliberates aloud with himfelf on the expediency of cutting his fon-in-law's throat, by which he (the father-in-law) muft become a gainer.

" If by his death the other were to marry my daughter,
" I fhould gain in him a powerful protector. who would
" raife me a hundred degrees higher than I am."

But above all, the character of Rodogune may be regarded as conftituting the infamy of the author, and the fuccefs of it that of

[3] " I would accept Livia's place of him,
" As a more certain means to compafs his deftruction."

the theatre; it is an affemblage of villainies, each more abominable than the reft, at once deftitute of caufe, connections, intereft, or probability. Horror itfelf degenerates into ridicule, becaufe the wickednefs of one of the two perfonages becomes the parody of the other: it is a mother, who while avowing, with extravagant refinements, to her fons, that fhe has with her own hand murdered their father, her hufband; tells them, that in order to be declared king by her, they muft, like her, commit parricide, and bring her the head of a princefs with whom fhe knows them to be paffionately enamoured: a conduct in her no lefs ridiculous than horrible[4]. This is the ferious piece, and here follows the parody.

The

[4] The idea of propofing to the lovers of Rodogune to put her to death by their hands, is abfurd; becaufe Cleopatra cannot ferioufly imagine that they will accede to her propofal; becaufe it is totally unneceffary; and becaufe it is imprudent. The old Megara has a thoufand other means to rid herfelf of the princefs fhe fears; and from the moment that fhe has difclofed to her fons this extravagant bargain, fhe muft expect that if they are not the minifters of her vengeance, they will take meafures to defeat it.

Mr. Voltaire has made thefe remarks in his commentary on Corneille, and though he wanted confidence not to praife the piece, he is, notwithftanding, charged with having malignantly

The young princefs informed of the propo-
fition made to her lovers, promifes in return to
beftow her hand on him who will bring her the
head of his mother.   I know not what apologift
of Corneille pretends to juftify this paffage;
becaufe, fays he, the bargain of Rodogune is a
mere fineffe; fhe knows very well that they will
not take her at her word.   It is in that very particular that it is the more abominable; and that
I can neither conceive how Corneille could give
birth to fuch a monfter, nor how the public
could applaud it.

Even that celebrated fcene in the 5th act, is
like the reft of the piece, but a feries of puerility
as well as horror.   The affaffination of the
youthful and vigorous Seleucus, in a little walk
of the garden, by the hand of an aged mother,
his death, which happens juft on the pronunci-
ation of the word, " It is ——" which prevents
his revealing the name of his murderefs; the
uncertainty of the good man Antiochus, divided

malignantly fought occafions for cenfure, and induftrioufly
laboured to leffen the tribute of applaufe.

One obfervation ought to have its place here, which is,
that Rodogune, the moft horrible and difgufting piece,
except Atrea, on the theatre, is likewife one of the worft
written, and moft deficient in plot and in conduct; fo much
was the genius of the author cramped, in being facrificed
to this abominable fpecies of writing.

between

between his young miftrefs and the antique fury
who has already boafted to herfelf of the parricide fhe has committed; that fwelling cheft,
and at laft the horrid purpofe of Megara, reduced to the neceffity of poifoning herfelf; her
blafphemies ftill more ridiculous than ufelefs, all
this is beneath even the moft barbarous æra of
the theatre.

If the name of Corneille and the buftle of
reprefentation did not influence us; if at the
prefent day we dared to eftimate according to its
real merit what our anceftors admired; and what
even we ourfelves have been long taught to efteem
from tradition; if we did not endeavour to
caft an illufion before us, by voluntarily dif-
guifing what we feel at this horrible fpectacle;
in miftaking for an emotion occafioned by the
grandeur and beauty of compofition, that
which refults from the ftage trick of actors, the
change of fcenery, and even the aftonifhment
into which we are thrown by a collection of
fuch abfurdities; Rodogune would be configned to the like oblivion as Theodore, Surena,
Pertharites, and fo many other pieces, the fruit
of the moft unequal genius perhaps, ever produced by nature : a man to whom it was allotted
never to be moderately good, or bad; and who

in

in the one is as much above his competitors, as he is beneath them in the other.

The decent, tender, and delicate Racine, uniting a superiority of taste with an equal share of expression and sentiment, took proper care not to stain his drama in like manner, by making of his principal personages, of those through whom he wished to excite the pity or admiration of his audience, such characters as *Brinvilliers*, or *Guilleris*, whom even ordinary justice must devote to the wheel or the stake.

A deference for the Greeks, and the prejudice of the age in which he lived, induced him to undertake Phædra; but he called forth all the powers of his genius to soften and modify this subject: perhaps he was to blame in having undertaken it : but it was impossible to palliate it with more art. He throws on the confidante the more odious part of the calumny which produces the catastrophe: he made it a species of virtue in Œnone, and was equally attentive to punish her for it.

If, in compliance with historical fact, he was obliged to describe Aggripina, the mother of Nero, both in conduct and expression, as a woman void of principle ; of putting into her mouth the same avowal as the Cleopatra of Rodogune, that of an attempt on her husband's life ; with what

L   delicacy

delicacy does he pafs over the painful and neceffary paffage :

> " He died—a thoufand rumors fpread to my difgrace,
> " I check'd the early news of his deceafe, &c."

We find in his pieces but two unpleafant characters of his own invention; two villains dif-
agreeable to behold, Narciffus and Mathan; but
thefe, in the firft place, are fubaltern characters,
and in the next, the author has taken due care
to compofe the fpectators by more confoling
contrafts; the generous Burrhus appears the more
noble, near the affociate of Locufta: the indulgent magnanimity of the warlike Abner becomes the more ftriking, when oppofed to the
daftardly cruelty of the high prieft.   If the latter
is bafe enough to fay, what fo many courtiers
think :

> " What matters it, ignoble blood to fpill?
> " Let us not load our king with ufelefs cares,
> " To be by him fufpected, ftands inftead of guilt."

The general of the army exclaims with horror,

> " Oh Mathan! is that fit language for a prieft?"

Whereas, in Corneille, the wildeft and moft
atrocious fentiments, have nothing to counterbalance them; the bafe and vindictive rage of
Emilia, Cinna, Cleopatra, and Rodogune, has
no contraft or oppofition.

This

This ſpecies of brutality, much eaſier to attain than the delicacy of Racine, has likewiſe
gained many more proſelytes : the pretended art
of poetry of the Greeks has been thought juſtified by the example and ſucceſs of Corneille :
our ſtage has ſince that period teemed with
atrocious ſpeculators, who perſuaded themſelves
that the moſt certain method of intereſting the
public, was to place before them ſcenes worthy
of the *Greve*, or of *Tyburn* ; they have infected
it with ſandalous epilepſies, given as the effect
of paſſions carried to their higheſt pitch ; and
unhappily ſometimes applauded. At the commencement of the preſent century in particular,
a man appeared, who after his ſecond tragedy,
was ſuppoſed to poſſeſs in an eminent degree the
talent of inventing refined villainies, of giving
birth to heroes whoſe crimes our moſt ſhameful
puniſhments were incapable of expiating : and
of this indeed he afforded us a terrible ſpecimen
in his Atrea.

This firſt eſſay it is true, inſtantly inſpired a
juſt horror : the poet never after dared to in-
dulge himſelf in ſuch ſhocking barbarities ; but
far from his docility gaining him applauſe, inſtead
of allowing him the credit due to his reformation,
it was not even remarked in him : he was ſtill
thought to retain the gloomy enthuſiaſm of which

he

he had been corrected; this error, by another
inconfiftency, became the groundwork of his
glory and fame. He was decreed the honors
due to the inventor of a new ftyle. He was
compared to the two mafters at that time
in poffeffion of the French theatre, and as the
town had without reflection, and contrary to
reafon and evidence, affigned to the one the
exclufive province of the fublime, and to the
fecond that of the pathetic; they decreed to the
third the excellence of the *fombre* and terrible: this
abfurd diftribution is ftill regarded as a juft one
by the public, though it is but neceffary to open
one's eyes to be made fenfible of its impropriety.

Be it faid at the prefent day, when there remains no more of Crebillon than his works,
when his pofterity is even extinct, and that in
appreciating his productions according to their
real merit, we run no rifk of hurting the feelings
of any one; that though he had actually poffeffed,
and was ftrongly impelled to a difplay of this horrible talent, it was by no means proper to fanction
it by applaufe. But he had it not, at leaft he
was contented with a fingle effort; as fince Atrea,
which, as I have aleady faid, was but the fecond
of his pieces, and may confequently be regarded
as his *debut*, he is no more *fombre* than any other:
he is only fomewhat more harfh in his ftyle, and
oftentimes

oftentimes but a little more ridiculous in his plans.

Pyrrhus, the beſt, or rather the leaſt infuffer-able of his pieces, prefents fcarcely any other than traits of virtue, there is not a drop of blood fpilled. Rhadamiſtus is a foolifh, rather than a wicked man : he defcribes himfelf as

" Virtuous without principle, vicious without defign."

" A foe to guilt; but yet no friend to virtue."

and accordingly he difcovers, till his death, nothing but inconfiſtency and irrefolution.

Eleⱥra is a puerile affemblage of uncon-neⱥed fcenes, of rage without objeⱥ and with-out grandeur ; it is a romance, which unites the extremes of infipidity and abfurdity. Even Clytemneſtra is nothing ; fhe appears in the piece but twice, the firſt time to load her daughter with abufe, the fecond to die with a jingle of words. In Semiramis, the plot is rather ridiculous than terrible, and the jargon of the Precieufes of Moliere, may appear as natural as that of the old Queen of Affyria, foolifhly in love with her own fon, whofe mother fhe does not indeed believe herfelf to be.

In fhort, in Idomeneus, Xerxes, Cataline, the Triumvirate, there is no more horror than genius. It is evident then, that the author was

L 3 indebted

indebted folely for his fame as a deep tragedian, or of a writer worthy of being regarded as a model in the terrible ftyle, to his Atrea; a fhocking performance it is true, but which, far from being a *chef d'œuvre* in a new fpecies, is but the laft degree of licentioufnefs and depravity, to which a ftyle already frightful in itfelf could defcend, and which ought to have been ftifled at its birth, rather than have been nurfed into maturity.

It is impoffible to conceive that there could ever exift in the human heart, more efpecially in youth, the idea of imagining, meditating on, and digefting fuch a plot; of fuperadding to the guilt which the Greek fable afcribes to the fons of *Tantalus*, the abominations with which the French piece is ftained: a baleful fpirit of revenge, nourifhed and concealed for twenty years, the fon of *Thieftes*, fupported during all this interval by the uncle as his own, with the defign of one day making him the affaffin of his father; the two fucceffive reconciliations, which are but the fame means of preparing, under two different forms, a double parricide; thofe fits of vengeance which efcape Atrea, at which a drunken Iroquois, departing to burn his enemy at the ftake, would blufh; and that anfwer impoffible to be qualified

in

in *Thieftes*, who not being able to doubt that his fon had been murdered, who beholding his blood before him, which he was about to drink, and whilft he touched the cup in which it was contained—hearing his brother afk him,

" Know'ft thou this blood ?"

replies in an epigram, in a play of words,

" I know my brother ?"

And this abominable conclufion of the piece,

" I now enjoy the fruit of all my crimes."

A verfe which fhocks us the more, becaufe in fact every thing has fucceeded with the monfter who pronounces it, and becaufe he quits the ftage in triumph. Do not thefe confiderations prove Atrea to be the fruit of a fcandalous madnefs, rather than a tragedy replete with terror ?

The author did not confider that the terrible, pufhed to fuch an excefs, becomes a puerility. An enraged grenadier, with a fabre in his hand, is without doubt an object of terror and alarm : but, if to make himfelf taller, he mounts upon ftilts ; if, in order to feem more enraged, he covers his face with an illumined mafk, he will then become a fcare-crow, and frighten

L 4 children ;

children only; his enormous ſtrides will but ſerve to render him the more ridiculous to the rational ſpectator. In like manner I think ſhould we have determined on Atrea, and the pretended *ſombre* of its author [s].

One might be led to believe that Crebillon was indebted for his fame in general, at firſt to the dearth which prevailed in the theatre when he appeared there, and afterwards to the neceſ-ſity under which hatred and jealouſy labored, for

---

[s] I recollect two lines of a piece I ſaw performed in my youth, very applicable to the ſubject. Previous to its re-preſentation, it had run through all the circles of Paris, read by the author according to cuſtom. The young poet, as uſual, was looked on as a new heir to Corneille and Racine, and as a competitor with Voltaire. His name already ſuf-ficiently famous, was about to eclipſe them all. The ſole embarraſſment was to aſſign him a department which was not already occupied by one of his predeceſſors. The public ſettled the difficulty by damning the piece, which was not even ſuffered to be finiſhed, like ſo many more honored with the like premature applauſe.

The couplet which in the readings had been moſt admired by the refined connoiſſeurs were theſe :

" Herod, to avenge an affront, would without remorſe
" See the blood of his laſt ſubject flow."

The pit was fired with indignation at this infernal ejacu-lation : it was received with univerſal execration and groans; but the audience have not always been actuated by the like equity, or political prudence.

want

want of a competitor, whom they might oppofe and prefer to Mr. Voltaire. It has been faid by fome, that the public was never, or at leaft but for a fhort time, the dupe of cabal, that it was foon undeceived in all kind of ill-founded prejudice, this example and a thoufand others prove the contrary. The public has, neverthelefs, in part done juftice to Atrea, by configning it to oblivion ; it has not done the like by Rodogune, becaufe the tafte of the people was not at that time formed, and that after all, Corneille, even in his extravagancies, ftill merited fome regard. It were to be wifhed that mankind may never more fuffer themfelves to be feduced by unnatural contorfions, which are ftill fometimes daringly prefented as fymptoms of grief, and that they will no longer endure the ftage, or the art of poetry, to be proftituted to licentious orgies, and bacchanalian fcreams, where they fhould be devoted to inftructive and pathetic forrow.

Mr. Voltaire feems to have feared to lay down the precept; but he has at leaft given the example. He has extended ftill further than Racine, that delicacy, the purity of which, ought ever to have been infeparable from thefe arts. He has none of thofe difgufting characters, none of that horror which excites indignation, even againft the

the author; he moves the heart and interefts the foul; he forces tears from his audience; he gives ufeful leffons, while employing no other refource than the reprefentation of calamities from which the pureft confcience cannot always preferve mankind, and honorable fentiments, which the paffions may fometimes combat, but which can never become extinct in virtuous minds.

Gufman, in Alzira, is harfh and haughty, but he is neither bafe nor cruel; Zamora, Alzira, Alvares, Monteza, are amiable, noble, and magnanimous; nor are they on that account the lefs interefting. The Duke de Foix is violent and even brutal; neverthelefs we can neither hate nor defpife him. Orbaffan, in Tancred, is humbled, but not debafed: Affur and Polifontes in Semiramis and Merope, are not very diftinguifhed characters, but they are not loaded with that guilt which gives pain to the beholder, or infpires him with horror and difguft. Polifontes and Semiramis are indeed blackened with guilt, but their crimes are long paft, nor do they form the fubject of the piece: their remorfe, the punifhment of the repenting wife in the one, and the maternal tendernefs of the other, are all that intereft in the reprefentation. In fhort, except Mahomet and Cataline (for I do not impute Œdipus to him, his firft effay, a

fubject

subject forced on him in his youth, and which was neither agreeable to his choice, nor to his taste,) except these two, there is not throughout all his tragedies, one part which can cause a blush in the actor who represents it; nor is this delicacy of less importance to genuine taste in literature, than to good order in society. And of these two exceptions, there is but one in which he is censurable. In Cataline, he was guided by history: he is reproachable rather in the choice of the subject, than in his mode of treating it: but Mahomet is wholly his own invention; and I own I cannot conceive that he should voluntarily, and contrary to historical truth, make a legislator, the founder of a great empire, of a religion still more extensive, vicious without object, cruel without a view, and a parricide without motive: he has elsewhere too loaded him with praise: what an idea, to repair to the theatre deliberately to tarnish a name venerated by one half of the globe, a character never yet reproached with one sanguinary act, no trick of deceit, except that of affirming himself sent from God; a false mission, but maintained by heroism and not by cruelty!

Add to this, that in this same piece, wherein the hero is so cruelly disfigured, the moral precept which the author proposes to deduce from

5   it,

it, is not more happily eſtabliſhed : neither is
the title of the tragedy juſtified, or the end ob-
tained. The view of the author is to excite our
abhorrence at the enthuſiaſm inſpired by fanaticiſm; and it is evident that fanaticiſm is in no
ſort the principle of the drama which bears the
title of it.

The murder committed by Zeide, is an effect
of military obedience, rather than religious zeal.
It is his General he obeys, not his God : he feels
remorſe : he imagines that he is committing a
crime, an idea which is inconſiſtent with fanaticiſm : the character and danger of this terrible
alienation of the mind, conſiſts in nothing more
ſtrongly than in the metamorphoſe it produces by
erecting crimes into virtues, and degrading virtues into crimes; an alarming faſcination which
has conducted ſuch characters as *Poltrot*, *Clement*,
Girard, *Diaz*, *Chatel*, &c. to the moſt ſhocking
actions with the calm of the pureſt conſcience.
This ſtate the author himſelf has happily de-
ſcribed in his Henriade.

He introduces the ſhade of the Duke de Guiſe,
encouraging the Dominican friar to the com-
miſſion of the crime; he recals to his remembrance the idea of his own murder, perpetrated
by Henry the third.

" Theſe

" Thefe wounds, Valois, by his affaffins made,
Punifh his perfidy, and pierce his heart ;
Shrink not at an affaffin's horrid name,
In thee 'tis virtue, tho' 'twas crime in him.

— — — — — —

The young reclufe, too eafily deceived,
Imagin'd he had heav'n's concerns in truft.

— — — — — —

Full of the fiend that had inflam'd his ire,
Devoutly he for parricide prepares.

— — — — — —

The foul of Clement happy, and at eafe,
Was with that confidence infpir'd, which none
But faints in perfect innocence enjoy."

This is fanaticifm, and affuredly Zeide has
nothing of it.

He fuppofes alfo that he is murdering a foe:
he is ignorant that it is his own father he is
about to put to death : had he known this; if,
while his arm was raifed, his birth had been revealed to him, and he had ftill perfifted to facrifice an idolater, if he had imagined he was
making a facrifice to his religion, not only by
trampling on the ordinary rights of humanity,
but even on thofe of nature, fanaticifm had then
appeared in all its fury and its danger; the
fpectacle would have been horrid.—True : but
the moral would have been ftriking : it would
perhaps have been an exception to the principle
I have

I have juft laid down, not to introduce too great a degree of atrocioufnefs on the fcene.

Laftly, This parricide even, this affaffination of Zopirus, by the hand of his fon, is, in the piece of which we are fpeaking, but a mere caprice in Mahomet, or rather in the author, and unfortunately a copy of Atrea, it has no conneftion with religion, it is no way neceffary, it is founded neither on probability nor expediency ; the manner in which it is conceived, condufted, perpetrated, and punifhed, is altogether unfkilful : but it is the only error of the kind with which Mr. Voltaire can be accufed ; nor does it prevent his title to the applaufe I have lately beftowed on him.

Add to this, what may ferve to excufe the one, and ftill further to juftify the other, that the charafter of Mahomet is poffeffed of grandeur ; he is not a mean and bafe villain, like Mathan, Narciffus, and Felix : take from the latter their turpitude and atrocioufnefs, nothing more remains of them ; whereas that of Mahomet, independent of this unneceffary murder, and ftill more ufelefs poifcning with which it is fullied, will ftill be interefting, and even grand.

However this may be, pofterity will find in the theatre of Mr. Voltaire, as in that of his predeceffors, after defeéts which will juftify criticifm,

criticifm, ftriking beauties, which will no lefs certainly enfure applaufe. The modern author. will probably be cenfured, in general, for the lamenefs of his plots, and above all the weaknefs of the principal incidents on which they turn. It will appear ftrange for inftance, that the plot of Tancred fhould confift wholly in: omitting the direction of a letter; it may feem inconceivable, that on ſuch a difcovery, Amenaide, the daughter of the moſt venerable knight of Syracufe, of the oldeſt chieftain of the ſtate, fhould be condemned on the ſpot, and led forth to punifhment, that fhe fhould entruſt no one, not even her father, with the ſecret which proves her innocence.

Gengifkan may perhaps appear little and pufillanimous, efpecially when contrafted with Idamea. The void which furrounds Semiramis may perhaps feem furprifing, a void but ill fupplied by Arzaces and Azema, whofe amours are neither fufficiently violent or complicated, to intereſt many fpectators. Pofterity will perhaps. be of opinion that the ghoft of Ninus is a prodigy wholly inefficient, and very far from being productive of confequences worthy of fo much parade; and that the poet having introduced it as a means of remedying the languor

of

of our theatre, ought to have given it more action and importance.

It will be faid, that it would not at firft have been fuffered, had he given it more force. I believe nothing of this, on the contrary I think that it is its infignificancy alone, which has rendered it ridiculous : I am of opinion, that had he given this fpectacle all the pomp and energy which it is capable of receiving, had the phantom before it appears to our view, been previoufly announced to us, by thofe hollow groans which are but hinted at in the piece ; if, inftead of appearing at the moment to order in vague terms a facrifice to his afhes, he had himfelf revealed the crime that was to be expiated, and poffeffed his fon with thofe facts which proved it ; if, inftead of affuming the puerile form of a man clothed in white, with his face covered with meal, that is to fay, in the abfurd and irrational attire we affix to an inhabitant of the other world, it had manifefted itfelf by fome external fign, by thofe attributes of terror which prevent or overwhelm reflection ; for inftance, by fuch a circumftance as is recorded in the hiftory of Daniel, of an illumined hand which traces flaming characters on the wall ; I doubt not but it would have met with the greateft fuccefs.

It

It is not eafy to forefee to which of his pieces pofterity will give the preference. He has already experienced at the hands of the public the fame felection, if we may ufe the term, to which Corneille and Racine have been doomed to fub-mit. All the pieces of the latter have main-tained their ground on the theatre, except three; one of which was never intended for it, and the two others are the production of early youth. Corneille is computed to have written at leaft thirty, of which fix or feven only have retained the honor of reprefentation. Mr. Voltaire, if I miftake not, has written twenty-four, whereof, to the beft of my recollection, nine have hithero conftantly fupported themfelves on the ftage.

It is from amongft thefe nine then, that we are to fix our choice, and if the election were mine, I fhould give it to Alzira: this piece feems to me to be in the theatre of Voltaire, what Iphigene is in that of Racine: the outlines of the two are very different, but their excellence, as it bears a relation to thofe which have gone before, and fucceeded them, appears to me to be pretty nearly the fame. I do not fay that Alzira is fuperior to Iphigenia, but I think the one the mafter-piece of Voltaire, as the other is that of Racine.

M   Before

Before I conclude this head, I think it in-
cumbent upon me to fay fomething in fupport of
my former decifion on Zara, a piece received
with fo much enthufiafm at its birth; the fuccefs
of which feems no ways impaired by time, a
piece of which the author has always fpoken
with fatisfaction, and hitherto inconteftably ranked
by his partizans among his beft productions.
I muft either juftify my opinion, or at leaft explain the grounds of it.

First, I think that the three firft acts of this
tragedy are cold, languid, unconnected with, and
even ufelefs to the piece : it can be faid to begin
but at the fixth fcene of the third, wherein Zara
evades the importunities of Orofmanes.

In the firft there is neither explanation nor
commencement of intereft, fince it relates only
to the marriage of the Sultan, and that this
marriage is not defcribed as capable of meeting
with the leaft difficulty.   The piece finifhes with
the order given to Nereftan to be out of the
dominions of Orofmanes the next day before
fun-rife.   We fee no reafon why this order fhould
not be executed.

And it would have been fo, but for a wink
given by Nereftan to young Odali; but this
refource appears to me an additional defect;
it would not even be perceived, if the author

4   had

had not caufed it to be taken notice of by
Orofmanes himfelf, by fuppofing in the latter a
prefentiment of jealoufy contrary to reafon.——
He could have no caufe to fear, or the audience
any ground to fuppofe, that Zara, whofe heart was
full of her lover, to whom fhe had lately made
the moft explicit declaration of her paffion, and
whom fhe had heard refufe her ranfom, that
Zara, who from the very firft fcene, has declared
that tendernefs in her foul would triumph over
the remaining feeble ideas of Chriftianity im-
planted in her youth, fhould refolve, from a nod
of the head, to incur every rifk, in order to
procure an interview with the Chriftian adven-
turer, whom the Sultan had in good humour
difmiffed : and neverthelefs if Nereftan returns
not, it is clear there can be no tragedy.

In the fecond act, the unexpected appearance
of Lufignan, and even the very romantic and
highly improbable recognition of him by Zara,
neither conftitutes a plot in the piece nor a commencement of interefts, fince we perceive no
danger to which Zara can be expofed from revealing the fecret of her birth; we feel that
Orofmanes is too generous and too deeply in
love, at hearing this, to give up his miftrefs
from a fcruple of religion.——A Sultan delicate
enough to difmifs his eunuchs, would not be

fo

fo timid as to hefitate marrying a pretty Chriftian, with whom he is violently enamoured, from
a fear of difpleafing his *Muftis*.

Befides he acquires an additional right to the
poffeffion of a conquered country, by an alliance
with the daughter of its former monarch. We can
only confider as a mere caprice in Lufignan, and
a proof of the embarraffment of the poet, that
verfe on which, notwithstanding, the whole piece
hinges:

> " O thou whom I dare not name,
> " Swear to keep fo fatal a fecret."

In fact, if Zara declares her name before Orofmanes, the tragedy ceafes.—Thus, at the end
of the fecond act, the audience is always perfectly eafy as to the fate of all the characters.—
In the third act, the exhortations, more violent
than chriftianlike, or pathetic, of Nereftan to his
fifter, his cruelty in infifting that fhe fhould be
baptized previous to her marriage, ftill prefent
nothing terrible, and the more fo, as after his
declaration that he fhall return foon to fee that
ceremony performed, and by confequence, as
this obftacle cannot continue for any length of
time, we continually expect to fee Zara and the
other characters delivered from their embarraffment by a confeffion of her birth.

The

The piece does not then in reality begin, till the scene where she refuses to comply with the earnestness of the Sultan, and requires a delay. But the part she acts in this is so weak, she fails so cruelly, and with an embarrassment so causeless, so ill justified by any apparent motive, and so ill expressed even poetically, to the generous Orosmanes; that she excites our indignation rather than our attachment; accordingly, we applaud the haughtiness of the lover, who has recourse to eastern manners, and orders " the doors of the seraglio to be for ever shut."

Here the plot, the danger, and the conflict of passions begin, and consequently the interest of the spectators; thus, in fact, the piece consists but of two acts, which are sustained by Orosmanes alone. Zara is continually indolent, silent, inanimate, and consequently uninteresting; but further, Orosmanes is but Roxana metamorphosed, which detracts considerably, if not from its impression on the theatre, at least from its merit to the reader.

And again, around Roxana what action, what passion, what a number of characters, all striking, all distinguished, and all worthy of the wishes and the admiration of the spectator! How great is Achmet! How pathetic is Atalida! How noble is Bajazet! How are all their interests united,

M 3 interwoven

interwoven together, if we may use the expreſſion; how do they exalt the character of the
Sultana without obſcuring it! But in Zara we
ſee but Oroſmanes; it is a print into which the
artiſt conveys but one figure of the grand picture
which he copied.

Laſtly, Zara is very feebly written; it is perhaps, of all Mr. Voltaire's pieces, written in the
moſt negligent ſtyle, which is the more ſurpriſing
becauſe although, if, as it is ſaid, he compoſed
it in eighteen days, he was thirty years in cor-
recting it; and that from the very nature of the
ſubject he ought to have made greater efforts to
approach the perfection of Racine in this, than in
any other performance.

But it will be aſked, how did it ſucceed at
firſt? How comes it ſtill to maintain its ground?
It is probable that its ſucceſs has been owing to
the circumſtance of an actreſs appearing in the
character who was then in all the ſplendor
of youth and beauty: the perſon and voice of
Mademoiſelle Goſſin gave birth to the illuſion;
a form and voice very different, as were thoſe of
Le Kain, ſerved to prolong it by varying its
object.

This actor, little indebted to nature, but
endowed with a powerful talent for performing
characters ſtrongly marked, gave equal energy

to

to the part of Orofmanes as that of Zara had received attractions from Mademoifelle Goffin. At the end of twenty years, it has fared with this fuccefs as with many others, the merit of which is not recurred to when it is once eftablifh-ed, as we may inftance in the character of Rodo-gune, which gives pleafure to none, and which all, notwithftanding, affect to admire.

OF

OF

Mr. VOLTAIRE's

COMEDIES.

———————

IT is to the Greeks that we are indebted for
Comedy as well as Tragedy; this ingenious
people, when they created the names of Melpomene and Thalia, affigned to each her feparate
department, and thefe were both equally licentious. If the former imagined the only means
of forcing tears were by dreadful horrors, the
fecond fought to excite our laughter by the moft
cruel fatire. Thus the defamation of the living,
or the dead, was the fole refource of the dramatic
art in its infancy.

It fhould feem that with fo near an affinity to
each other, thefe two branches might have been
cultivated by the fame hand : what I have before
obferved of the compatibility of oppofite talents
uniting in the fame man, appears to me incapable

of

of contradiction : I could have supported this theory by many other examples taken from the ancients, but, by a strange contradiction, those two species, the union of which seemed apparently most easy, are precisely such as never existed among them : the art of introducing characters on a stage, discoursing in dialogue, and of depicting, by their attitude and their expressions, the secret emotions they feel, has ever remained divided at Rome and at Athens, into two distinct departments.

In an age when warriors studied eloquence, when the most profound philosophers and the severest legiflators became the rivals of Æsop and Anacreon, in the composition of moral fables, or licentious ballads; the author, who in a dialogue entitled Tragedy, represented Phædra inflamed with a violent and miserable passion, Theseus at once credulous and jealous, Hippolitus haughty and unfeeling, never imagined it possible that he could have successfully delineated the same picture in a piece called Comedy : two words which had no manner of relation to what they signified. And on the other hand, Aristophanes, Menander, Plautus, or Terence, seemed to feel no inducement to entwine the wreaths of Melpomene with those of Thalia.

Most

Moft affuredly this fcruple, or this timidity, is not founded in the nature of things, or in any inability of the poets. It is an inconfiftency, whereof examples are not uncommon; and for which it is impoffible at the prefent, perhaps at any time, to affign any fufficient reafon.

The Spaniards, as I faid before, confounded thefe two fpecies of compofition, or rather they were unacquainted with either of them. Their pieces are as far from Sophocles or Terence as from Ariftophanes and Euripides. They, not-withftanding, adopted the general name of Comedy for all kinds of dramatic dialogue, whether humorous or pathetic, it was always the *Comedia famofa.*

Our firft poets, as I have remarked, being no other than their difciples, or rather their copyifts, gave no other title to their works, whatever was the fubject of them, Oroondates and Ameftris, as well as the Vifionaries or the Pedant, were alike deemed comedies. Mad. de Sevigné never gives any other name to the dramatic works of Corneille than that of comedy, and he had then produced all his good pieces: fhe gives the like title to thofe of Racine, after Andromache, Iphigenia, and Bajazet. The term of tragedy even at prefent is unknown in Spain and Italy, and it is of very recent date in France.

It

It is no way furprifing then, that the modern candidates for theatric fame fhould have retained the privilege of pafling from one of thefe departments to the other of them. The obfcene Hauteroche was not deterred from writing a tragedy, as bad indeed and as infipid as his comedies, excepting only one, are filthy and difgufting, The affected Marivaux has likewife attempted the bufkin, in common with many more: but generally fpeaking, few have gained any applaufe from the attempt.

The Liar of Corneille has alone remained on the theatre, and that is confidered as a model. Racine has written but one comedy; which is extremely amufing: it is only to be lamented that the effence of it evaporates, as we may fay, in the reprefentation, or cloys from the labour which the actors give it. Mr. Voltaire has availed himfelf of the like talent, but is it with equal fuccefs?

Doubtlefs we might have expected, that the man of his age who was beft acquainted with pleafantry and even with fatire, who when he was fo difpofed has pourtrayed the vices and follies of his fellow-creatures with the greateft ftrength, energy, and grace, in direct terms, would have been equally fuccefsful in exhibiting them perfonified, as we may fay; when the vivacity of action

was

was fuperadded to the livelinefs of ftyle; and this might have been with greater reafon expected of Mr. Voltaire, as he devoted himfelf to this labour at an age when his tafte had attained its greateft perfection, when he was the moft perfect mafter of ftyle and the choice of his fubject; when experience muft have completely initiated him into the intricacies of fociety, which he lafhed in the ftrongeft and moft pointed manner in his other writings. Neverthelefs he was no longer the fame, when defirous of affuming that office in dialogue.

In his romances, in his tales, in his difcuffions, apparently of the moft ferious nature, we meet with fallies which excite burfts of laughter, or fly ftrokes of wit, which afford a more refined, though a lefs fenfible gratification; but his comedies are very far from poffeffing either of thefe excellencies.

It is true there are three which are ftill retained on the ftage, and which we fee exhibited with pleafure, the Prodigal, Nanette, and the Scotch Woman, but thefe are more properly affecting romances than comedies. They have kept their ground by thofe ferious paffages of philofophical, moral, or fentimental matter with which they abound. Euphemon, Eliza, Nanette, are far from exciting gaiety: even Freeport, who in a

great

great meaſure decided the fate of the Scotch
Woman, is not lively, though poſſeſſed of dignity: and Waſp is more horrid, baſe, and diſguſting, than comic. An immoderate deſire of
revenge in the author, has cauſed him to lay
aſide that ſcrupuloſity, politeneſs, and candour,
which prevented him from ſullying his tragedies
with ſimilar characters.

In general, the few pleaſantries hazarded by
Mr. Voltaire in all his pieces, which are entitled
comedies, are of a very inferior caſt, more
nearly approaching to the forced burleſque of
Scarron, than the nature and gaiety of Moliere.
Even the Prodigal, M. Rondon, Fierenfat, are not
ſo diſtant from Don Japhet as may be ſuppoſed.

The falſe taſte which makes Don Japhet, and
whatever reſembles it, inſupportable, is an affected
ſearch after ludicrous terms, an effort to ſupply
by a pretended play of words the deficiency of
an author incapable of throwing pleaſantry into
the ſituation or the ideas; and this is the more
diſguſting in the Prodigal, as that piece is full
of pathetic traits excellently written, in which
grandeur is combined with the moſt affecting
ſimplicity.

It is ſtill worſe in the other comedies of Mr.
Voltaire, when he is deſirous of making his
ſpeakers humorous. In ſupport of this aſſertion, it
would

would be eafy to multiply extracts * which would juftify me in the ftrange comparifon I have juft made between him who, when he pleafed, was the moft polifhed and elegant wit, the moft exact obferver of decency of the prefent century, and the moft obfcene, infipid, and difgufting buffoon of the beginning of the laft.

Again, one cannot recover from the aftonifh-ment into which we are thrown, at beholding a writer of the moft exquifite tafte, I repeat it, who poffeffed in the greateft degree the *ton* of good company, who even gave it to thofe of his time; he, who in all his other writings difcovered the utmoft delicacy, grace, and eafe, who has moft fuccefsfully, and with a delicacy peculiar to himfelf, expofed in other writers the breaches they committed againft decency and propriety, miftake for theatrical humour that ftiffnefs of ftyle, that ftale pedantry, or thofe rebufes and grofs equivoques, too nearly bordering on puns, fo juftly profcribed in all genteel circles, and which at the prefent day would be fcarcely tolerated in the lower ranks of fociety.

Thefe, it will be faid, were the recreations of a great man. Lelius and Scipio amufed them-felves in making ducks and drakes; true, but

* The author has in fact given feveral, but as they turn chiefly on verbal allufions, they cannot well be rendered in another language.

they

they did not make the public witnefs to thefe amufements of their leifure hours.

And what feems ftill more incredible, is that Mr. Voltaire fhould be fond of this low ftuff, he introduces it fometimes even into his profe, and under his own name: let us confefs it at once, and have done with it. When his bile was once kindled, he indulged himfelf in this contemptible ribaldry; at the beft only worthy of Scarron or Rabelais, or rather of Father Garaffe, whom he has fo violently condemned.

When reproaching the decree of the Sorbonne againft Bellifarius, he attributes it to a Bachelor of Divinity, becaufe the word is commonly enough ufed in fchools. He calls M. L'Abbé Riballier, *Ribaudier*; he fometimes makes of Sabatier, *Savatier*, fometimes *Sabctier*; of Gayan, *Coyon*, and all this he prints. Thefe allegories, to ufe his own language towards Father Garaffe, differ fomewhat from thofe of Virgil and Ovid, and I cannot fee, whilft he indulged himfelf in the ufe of them, how he could impute it as a crime in the Jefuit to have called Theophilus a calf, becaufe his family name was Veau.

Let us blufh at this weaknefs which I have here mentioned, becaufe it is eftablifhed beyond all queftion by public documents, and rather not to have appeared to diffemble, than to force

it

it into notice. Let us lament that Mr. Voltaire either had not himself, or did not confult with friends poffeffed of the requifite delicacy, and fufficiently tenacious of his reputation, to caution him againft fuch an abufe of his talents. It were to be wifhed that there may be one day found an editor of his works bold enough to expunge thefe diftreffing blemifhes. I am even of opinion, that in fuppreffing all his comedies, except thofe which are ftill performed, the lofs would be fcarcely perceptible. They poffefs neither in defign, or digreffion, any thing worthy of regret.

The firft and the laft pieces of Corneille it is true are always printed together with thofe of his happieft moments, but the difparity is far lefs apparent. This great man is often a prodigy of genius, but never a model of tafte. For a contrary reafon it feems, we ought to fave Mr. Voltaire's enlightened readers the pain of fuch paffages as are unworthy of him, and from thofe who are not fo we fhould remove the danger of paffing them over unperceived.

OF

MR. VOLTAIRE's

FUGITIVE,

AND OTHER

POETICAL PIECES.

HITHERTO I have adventured to criti-
cize, and dare believe that the impartial
reader will equally acquit me of unmerited cenfure
as ill founded applaufe; but juftice now confifts in
admiration. If aught can redeem the inconceivable weaknefs of Mr. Voltaire's comedies, it muft
doubtlefs be his fugitive pieces; a fpecies of writing in which he has no fuperior, and fcarcely any
equal. In the midft of labors, apparently the
moft foreign from fuch a purfuit, he cultivated this
airy kind of literature; he enriched it, feemingly
without thinking of it, with an infinite variety of
pieces, all varied, and fparkling with wit, tafte, and
knowledge—it was Phidias, who while at work

N 2   on

on the Olympian Jupiter, ftrewed the floor of
his work-fhop with fragments of ivory and gold.

Under this head I comprehend that multitude
of little pieces on every fubject, which flowed from
him without effort, and which feemed to coft him
no more than a madrigal—fuch as tales wherein
variety and ornament are blended with gaiety;
epiftles, fatires, and above all treatifes in verfe;
productions of his happieft moments—of that
period when he laboured with the greateft care—
when the apprehenfion of enemies, ever prone
to cenfure, preferved him from the negligence
into which confidence and habitual fuccefs afterwards betrayed him; in all thefe feveral kinds of
compofition, his name will ever be ranked amongft
the moft celebrated, and will often be regarded
as the firft.

Not that he has written as many fatires as
Boileau, or as many tales as La Fontaine; but
amongft thofe of the former, how few are there
really worthy of their author? And to the tales
of the latter may we not fuccefsfully oppofe the
Poor Devil, and the Ruffian at Paris? It will
be faid that the ftyle is different. Doubtlefs it
is; if they were copies could they be compared?

The Poor Devil abounds too much in per-
fonalities, and they are too harfh; this again is
granted: *Griffet* is cruelly lampooned in it, and

he

he had never injured the author. I acknowledge it—I do not excufe the latter; it is one of his greateft defects—but were *Quinalt, Burfaut,* or *Hainaut* more criminal towards the modern Juvenal? The queftion here refts; not on the moral, but literary merit of thefe pieces.

With regard to epiftles, does not Mr. Voltaire, who has inconteftably the advantage in point of number, poffefs it likewife in that of variety, agreeablenefs, and perhaps of utility? Under this title I include his feven treatifes on Moderation, on the Nature of Man, &c. Has Boileau ever written finer verfes than thefe?

> " Can Sylva's felf th' œconomy explain,
> Which works digeftion, and makes food fuftain ;
> How the bile through fo many channels flows !
> How, by degrees, 'tis filtrated, and goes
> To pour into my veins a purple tide,
> By which both ftrength and fpirits are fupply'd ;
> Which makes the pulfe of life inceffant beat,
> And makes the brain intelligence's feat ?"

The author of the Lutrin congratulates himfelf on having, as he faid in profe, happily enough fatyrifed the Peruque. Would he not with more juftice have applauded the preceding defcription, had it been his own?

Shall we find in any poet, or in any language, many paffages fuperior to thofe which occur in

N 3

the

the Treatife on the Equality of Conditions among Men?

Whilft, like Boileau, he treated moral and ufeful fubjects with dignity, Mr. Voltaire intermingled philofophy and gaiety in his epiftles, which Boileau did not; he likewife enriched them by defcriptions of the manners of the world, by mafterly and juft traits, worthy of Moliere; which redoubles my aftonifhment when I reflect on his comedies.

For inftance, in his epiftle entitled the Life of Paris and Verfailles, he introduces two women vifiting each other.

> " Vifits her friend, in pomp and ftate,
> Afcends, and then repents too late,
> Embracing yawns, and plain is feen
> In her conftrain'd behaviour, fpleen;
> She feems to beg for nonfenfe gay,
> To make her languor pafs away;
> They interchange fome faint careffes,
> They talk of weather, plays, and dreffes;
> Of fermons, and of ribbons price,
> And are exhaufted in a trice.
> Now through neceffity grown dumb,
> A tune they both begin to hum;
> But Mr. Abbé enter'd foon,
> Prieft, gallant, fharper, and buffoon;
> Endow'd with various talents rare,
> Who for fome months was mafter there.
> A formal coxcomb enter'd too,
> Pleas'd in the glafs himfelf to view;

I   Both

Both pedants pleas'd, their jargon suits—
. A captain enters; both are mutes."

How can we reconcile it, that he who had so
happily caught these impreffions, who was thus
able to exprefs them in foliloquy, when fpeaking
in the firft perfon, fhould be incapable of animating them in dialogue, of affigning them a
language correfponding to their actions ? It is,
that generally fpeaking, on the theatre as in epic
poetry, all he knew, all he was capable of, was
to defign a figure, he was unable to give it
animation.

In his Epiftles on Agriculture, who can read
unmoved thofe verfes addreffed to a *petit maitre,*
who thinks it impoffible to live any where but
amidft the buftle and pleafures of the world.
It were endlefs to point out paffages of this
nature; and befides, the works where they are
to be met with, are too well known to render it
neceffary.

As to the art of narration, in the *naiveté* of
his fables, and the fprightlinefs of his tales,
wherein confifts the principal merit of La Fontaine, he is far from being equal throughout ; but
in his choice paffages he is enchanting. *Ce qui
plait aux dames Gertrude, les trois Manieres,* &c.
with a different kind of merit, muft they not be
allowed that, of affording infinite pleafure ?

N 4   I re-

I remember having formerly heard Mr. Voltaire reproached, with having taken his *Fee Ur-
gulle* from the Englifh Chaucer if I miftake
not; but has La Fontaine invented even one of
his fubjects? Is he not indebted to Æfop, to
Phædrus, &c. for the ground of his fables, and
for that of his tales to the Queen of Navarre,
to Boccace, and from that Canon from whom fo
little edifying is to be gained, who compiled the
Moyen de parvenir?

Another criticifm, as ill founded as the laft,
is that which recurs to me on the *Trois Manieres:*
this idea it is faid, is pillaged from the *Daughters
of Mineus of La Fontaine.* Which is faying,
that the poet of the 18th century has entered the
lifts againft him of the 17th; true—but what do
they poffefs in common? Nothing—but having
each written a piece containing three ftories; one
of them pathetic, another humorous, and a third
of a compofite nature—but Raphael has painted
the Holy Family; and Rubens the Jordans; can
thefe be deemed plagiarifts, becaufe they have
both introduced Virgins attending on Jefus and
St. John? Orofmanes is really an enfeebled
copy, but the *Trois Manieres,* though twice defcribed, are, notwithftanding, both originals.

If Mr. Voltaire be thus capable of maintaining, without difadvantage, the comparifon between

4

thefe

thefe two juftly celebrated poets, how great is
his fuperiority when compared with Voiture,
Chapelle, Chaulieux, and Piron. He rifes fuperior to all in the number of his pieces, and
to each of them in eafe and fprightlinefs;
he continually prefents us with ingenious fimilies,
and allufions at once poignant and inftructive:
we difcover in them the delicacy and lightnefs
of the man of the world, united with the dignity
and eafe of the philofopher; and what, as I have
already obferved, is not always to be found in
his Tragedies or Henriade, the correctnefs of
expreffion keeps pace with that of thought.

The little which remains to us of Voiture is
buried in the multiplicity of infipidities with
which he abounds, and which have had as great
a run, and have equally contributed to his reputation with thofe pieces which can bear the ordeal
of good tafte: it is the fame with de Chapelle.

I open Chaulieu, that Chaulieu fo celebrated
by Voltaire himfelf; I do not find a fingle piece
fuftained throughout, not one copy of verfes wherein the poet, either fatigued or carelefs, did not
appear to hold his readers in contempt, or feemed
to have forgotten that he wifhed to make, or
thought he was making verfes. One of his beft
epiftles, is that on the death of the Marquis de

la

la Fare; and in this we meet with many lines in rhyme, which are not even tolerable profe.

I open alfo the collection of Piron's works, a poet of reputation, efpecially for the lighter kind of productions, whofe name one dramatic work alone has affifted, or eftablifhed; but well known for his epigrams and convivial fallies, ftill more than by his *Metromania*. See his manner of addreffing women—women to whom he owed refpect and gratitude, in his madrigal addreffed to Mad. de Tencin, the Geofrin of her time.

It is well known that fhe gave the literary men who were ufed to meet at her houfe the name of " her beafts;" a title fufficiently droll, and expreffive of very little efteem on either fide. To thefe beafts fhe was accuftomed every year to make a prefent of a pair of velvet breeches. Piron one day fent her a ftraw-hat, accompanied with this epigram, the point of which, if it may be faid to poffefs any, confifts in the moft difgufting groffnefs : compare it with the madrigals of Mr. Voltaire, and then form an opinion.

The only cenfure to which the latter is juftly liable in thefe productions, is fomewhat too much monotony in many of his fugitive pieces; too ftrong an aptitude, as I have already faid, to beftow praife, whether on the great, whom he feared, or men of letters, whofe good opinion he wifhed

to

to conciliate; this spirit reigns so strongly through-out these eulogiums, that they rarely seem sincere, and still less often are they just; but what signi-fies this to posterity? Who now interest them-selves in the enquiry whether Glycera was as pretty, and Canidia as ugly as Horace pretends? And will the greater part of those, thus im-mortalized by Mr. Voltaire, be better known than Glycera and Canidia?

PART

PART the SECOND,

OF

Mr. VOLTAIRE's

PROSE WORKS.

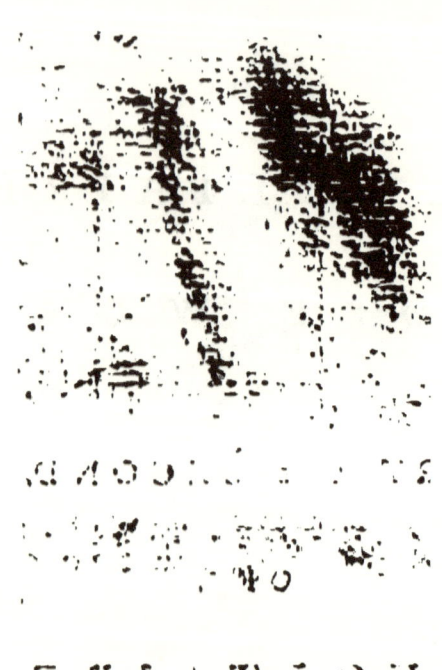

OF

MR. VOLTAIRE's

PROSE WORKS,

THIS is the field in which Mr. Voltaire might be truly faid to triumph; at leaft, the applaufe he gains or forces from his readers, when addreffing them in a language divefted of the pomp, the pretenfions, we may even fay the embarraffments of poetry, is then much lefs liable to exception. A purity of elocution, a juftnefs of epithet, a profufion of ideas, perfpicuity and energy of expreffion, neatnefs of ftyle, and harmony of period, gaiety, dignity, all are here found, united with an eafe, a facility, and an art of familiarizing every fubject, in a manner before him unparalleled.

I have heard it much regretted by fome enlightened men, whofe opinion I think it an honor to adopt, that, after producing Tancred,

he

he had not abandoned poetry in general, and efpecially that of the theatre, in order to devote himfelf wholly to hiftorical and philofophic profe, retaining at moft for his amufement but the lighter fpecies of poetry, which, except in the mechanical habit of rhyme, coft him no pains whatever. They contend, that this author would have acquired more extenfive fame had he adopted this idea, had he only increafed his profaic works with an equal number of excellent productions, as he has fwelled the lift of his tragedies with feeble pieces, which, though brought forth with lefs labor, reflect lefs credit on his memory.

I fay, that this labor, to which he has given too evident a preference, would have coft him lefs: nothing is more certain. I fhall not enter here into a formal difquifition on the merits or demerits of thefe two fpecies of compofition, nor inveftigate deeply whether it be more laborious for a writer to be fubjected to the rules of poetry; which, though they may fometimes cramp his genius, more frequently fupport and aid him in concealing his weaknefs; than to form a ftyle of his own, wherein, as he can have no other guide than a juft tafte and a good ear, his judges are the more rigid, as they are not to be mifled by a laboured harmony—where fuc-

cefs

cefs is not enhanced by having furmounted difficulty, nor a failure of it palliated in having
had it to oppofe. Perhaps it might not be fo
difficult to prove as is generally imagined, that
the apparent freedom of the one ftyle is no more
compatible with moderate genius, than the real
fervitude of the other.

Eminent profe writers are at leaft as fcarce as
eminent poets. In Greece the latter title is beftowed on Homer, Hefiod; Pindar, Simonides,
Anacreon, Theocritus, Æfchylus, Sophocles,
Euripides, Ariftophanes, Menander, Cratefepo-
lis, and feveral others. We find Herodotus,
Thucydides, Xenophon, Plato, Ariftotle, Demofthenes, and, in a later age, Polybius and
Plutarch, are all who have been honored with
the former epithet. Again, in feveral of thefe,
it is the fubject we admire, more than the ftyle:
they are judicious authors, rather than models
of fine writing.

The age of Auguftus offers us Lucretius,
Terence, Plautus, Virgil, Horace, Ovid, Ca-
tullus, Tibullus, Martial, Juvenal, Lucan, &c.
deemed, though with different degrees of merit,
the flower of Latin poetry; in the profe of that
language we have but Titus Livy, Cicero, Salluft, Tacitus, the two Plinys, and Seneca, which

at leaft, in point of number, do not make an equal balance.

Look alike into the literature of all nations who have cultivated the fine arts, and have any pretenfions to fame, whether in poetry or eloquence; we fhall find by the fame fingularity, that thofe who have moft diftinguifhed themfelves in that kind of compofition wherein a difplay of genius feemed moft difficult, are in point of number, at leaft equal, and oftentimes fuperior, to fuch who have confined themfelves to one, feemingly moft eafy. Appearances then muft have been fallacious in this matter; and it fhould appear that the practice of one of thefe idioms muft at leaft be fubject to as many difficulties as the other.

Still further, may we not fay, that poetry is in fome fort the infantine language of the human mind? It is in verfe that it lifps its feeble efforts, incapable of expreffing itfelf in profe, till arrived at its full maturity and ftrength. Look into the hiftory of the origin of all nations, of every code of legiflation, and fyftem of philofophy, you will find poets and verfes in the firft dawnings of civilization.

Homer preceded Herodotus, and Orpheus, Linus, and many other poets, had preceded Homer.

Homer. Ennius wrote the annals of Rome in hexameter verfe, before any one thought of digefting them into the language of common intercourfe." Mofes, the firft profe writer of his country, has preferved in Canticles, hymns compofed by himfelf, in a meafure of which he was not the inventor. The Hebrews then had their Orpheus alfo before their Herodotus.

Among ourfelves, did not our whole ftock of literature for a long time confift of rude romances, peices compofed of barbarous verfes, but in meafure, and fubject to rhythmical quantity, and returning rhymes? The newly difcovered favages, who could fcarcely be faid to have any language or fociety, and no writing, had, notwithstanding, their jugglers, conjurers, and poets.

May we not hence conclude, that poetry is the expreffion moft natural to man, and confequently the eafier; and that a dignified, elegant, and fublime profe, fuch as that of great writers muft neceffarily be, is in reality the perfection of language; fince the latter cannot be acquired till the former has attained its full maturity?

Laftly, there is a third confideration, of no lefs weight if the queftion were to be ferioufly difcuffed, which is, that among the moderns at leaft, all the diftinguifhed profe writers defirous

of

of becoming poets, have fucceeded in the attempt; whereas it is but rarely that the beft
poets have, with labor, even been able to produce any tolerable profe.

This remark, it is true, will hold good with
refpect to the moderns only; among the ancients, by a continuance of the fame abfurdity
which I have already remarked feemed to have
entirely feparated the provinces of tragedy and
comedy, we do not find that poetry and profe
were ever cultivated by the fame hand : none of
thofe names I have enumerated are to be found
in both lifts. Hiftorians, fo little fcrupulous in
other points, in fuch like frauds, have never
dreamed of attributing any treatife in profe to
Scipio or Lelius, who were attached to verfe,
and were fufpected of having a fhare in Terence's
works. We have fome obfcene epigrams attributed to the celebrated ufurper who founded
the empire of the Cæfars; but he has not left a
line of profe; there exifts not even a madrigal
attributed to the real Cæfar, Livy, Salluft, Tacitus, or Cicero, to all thofe profe writers who
conftitute the glory of Roman eloquence.

But in our languages, which are formed from
a mixture of the barbarous idioms of the North
with thofe of Greece and Rome, it has been
otherwife. If Cervantes and Machiavel are not

at

at the head of the poets of their respective nations, as they are models to them in prose writing, they have notwithstanding succeeded on the
theatre, and consequently are no strangers to this
division of poetical empire. Addison, one of
the authors who has most contributed to ennoble
the English prose, has likewise enriched the London theatre with one of its best pieces, and several operas. Milton, the Homer of Great-
Britain, is one of its most prolific prose writers,
if not one of its most esteemed.

In France, all those celebrated romance writers, who were at first deemed the honor of our
literature, and who at present seem, perhaps contrary to all reason and justice, to be considered
the disgrace of it, Calpremede, Gomberville,
Scuderi, Durier, Desmarets, Voiture, &c. have
with the greatest facility passed from one department to the other, and they began with making
rhymes; versification and the drama were the
amusement of their youth; it was reserved for a
maturer age to develope a taste and a talent for
prose.

Moliere, Hamilton, La Motte, Fontenelle, and
a thousand others, have possessed this two-fold
faculty, and with the like success, but always in
such a way as to make it apparent, that prose was
the real and serious empolyment of their talents,

O 3 and

and that the moſt laboured poetical productions were an amuſement to them.   Is it not ſtrange that Corneille, Boileau, La Fontaine, J. B. Rouſſeau, ſo ſuperior each of them in the ſeveral kinds of poetry to which they were attached, ſhould have ſunk even beneath mediocrity, when deſirous of making excurſions into her ſiſter's kingdom, reputed of ſuch eaſy acceſs.

Racine is the only one, not, who as it is ſaid, gathered the double palm before Mr. Voltaire, but who from lofty poetry could deſcend to proſe with grace and eaſe; the only one whoſe genius has preſerved the ſame excellence in the labored decoration of the pretended language of the gods, and the grand ſimplicity of the real language of man.

Is it not poſſible to account for this ſingular fact, to aſſign ſome cauſe for the apparently limited powers of the one, and the contradictory fecundity of the other? I am about to hazard a poſition, which, to the enthuſiaſtic inexperience of youth, may appear a blaſphemy, but from which reflection will ſoon diſperſe the ſcandal, and even juſtify thoſe aſſertions, hazarded without proof in this philoſophic age, by men, with whom, in other reſpects, I am no way ſolicitous to hold a community of principles.

The

The verſification of every language is but a habit.—It is the idea which conſtitutes poetry, it is rule which makes verſes: the latter then is mechanical, wherein practice alone is neceſſary to enſure ſucceſs. A child, who was early accuſtomed to expreſs himſelf in hexameter or alexandrine verſes, whether inſtructed in French or Latin, would find no more difficulty in faſhioning his ordinary language to this meaſure, than we find in uſing that which we have learnt from our nurſes.

I remember having formerly been acquainted with a company of intelligent young people, who had impoſed this law on themſelves when they met together; and though their meetings were but twice, and oftentimes but once a week, and conſequently their habit of rhyming was but ill kept up; they had notwithſtanding acquired ſuch a facility in the practice, that they often made thirty or forty verſes ſucceſſively, and expreſſed whatever they had to ſay in this manner. Some of their lines, as may be ſuppoſed, were moſt execrable; but there eſcaped them often very aſtoniſhing ones.

If any thing ſurpriſes me in the extempore ſpeakers of Italy, it is, that they are ſo rare. In a richer, more flexible, and leſs confined language than our own, I ſhould conceive it poſ-

ſible

fible, with fome little labor and practice, to
acquire an habitual meafure like rhyme, fo as
to be able to command it at the precife moment
without trouble or difficulty.

As to the poetry of compofition, that which
confifts in grandeur of images and livelinefs of
defcription, it is quite another matter; this is
what labor and habit never can give, and what
genius alone can beftow: but does this talent,
which forms what we call a poet when expreffed
in methodical founds, modulated by rules and
according to certain received principles, differ
from that which manifefts itfelf in the fpeech of
an orator, by the fame founds differently modi-
fied; or that which in the head of a philofopher,
or an hiftorian, difcovers itfelf in ideas rendered
fenfible through the means of the fame words,
arranged only with lefs art, and clothed in more
fimple ornaments? I think not.

The orator may hazard a greater number of
images, he may difplay greater boldnefs than the
two laft, the poet may allow himfelf a ftill wider
latitude, becaufe the ftyle of each is different: it
is tafte that points out to them feverally, the degree of embellifhment or force which fhould accompany their ideas, and the various forms under
which they are to give birth to that enthufiafm,
that development of ideas, which is termed genius,

and

and which at bottom is abfolutely the fame
in all.

Thus moderate men, defirous only of taking
exercife, walk quietly along, without fatiguing
themfelves; he who has urgent bufinefs on his
hands makes greater hafte, regardlefs of difcovering a ftronger agitation in his deportment; a man impelled by violent paffion, or
actuated by powerful intereft, runs with ftill
lefs conduct, he rufhes onward, and exhaufts
his whole ftrength in the purfuit: all three make
a different ufe of their legs, though in all, it is
by the fame organ, and the like principle of
motion.

Now, if as the fact proves, contrary to probability, and in fome fort contrary to reafon,
the one apparently the more difficult, is the eafier,
in this kind of mental labor; if the fonorous
fcaffolding with which a poet is furrounded, and
whereon he fupports himfelf, is in reality but
the refult of habit, foreign from genius, and
better adapted to conceal a want of talents, than
to facilitate their birth; ought we to be embar-
raffed to explain how thofe fuperior geniufes
amongft ourfelves, who at an early period have
attached themfelves to this habit, were afterwards incapable of eftranging themfelves from

it,

it, and seem to have sunk beneath their own
level when desirous of descending from it.

Take two children of unequal constitutions,
constrain the more robust from daring to take
a step without assistance, compel him to uphold
himself in every motion by a support from which
he cannot escape; whilst the other, permitted to
preserve his independence, shall make a free use
of those resources with which nature has endowed him: the first, when he wishes to detach
himself from his machinery, will never be able
to acquire the easy unconstrained deportment of
the second, who on the other hand, from caprice or amusement, will soon have adopted the
secret shackles of the other. This is the reason
why, and the manner in which, in our modern
idioms the talent of writing a fine prose, has
often been united with one for poetry, whilst examples of this union in celebrated poets are so
rare.

Amongst the ancients, another reason may be
assigned, for the division constantly maintained
between these two departments of literature.
Perhaps the mechanism of their verse, founded
on a different principle in their language, on
another conformity in their verse, was a more
real and sensible obstacle to those excursions which
had united them.

In

In Greek and Latin every word has not only its harmonic power, as we may fay, and the time of its mufical duration determined by certain laws which cannot be infringed, but there are many words excluded from poetry by the nature and the arrangement of the fyllables which compofe them; others again take a fenfe in verfe which they have not in profe. The reader accommodated himfelf to thefe flights, which oftentimes became even beauties; but the poet, in quitting one of thefe diftricts, with the refources and limits of which he was thoroughly acquainted, perhaps knew nothing of the other but its barrennefs, without even fufpecting its fertility, from being unaccuftomed to it.

Our modern languages have neither this profody, this latitude, or this privation; there are no words neceffarily excluded from our poetry by the number and conftruction of the letters and fyllables of which they are compofed. The famous *Effe videatur* of Cicero, or its equivalent, would in Italy, England, Spain or France, be alike proper to a poet, and an orator; but in neither of thefe idioms would it be allowable to call, as Virgil has done, the noife a horfe makes when running a quadrupedtal found; nor, like Homer, the fmile of a woman bathed in tears a crying laugh. Neither Cicero nor Demofthenes, when

when speaking the same language, would have ventured on such picturesque expressions, reserved alone amongst them, for that species of literature which has dared to adopt them.

In like manner the words *Virgo*, *Puella*, are applied by Virgil to married women. He says of Pasiphae, already a mother,

" Ah virgo infelix quæ te dementia cepit ?"

Of Euridice, wife of Orpheus,

" Immanem ante pedes moritura puella
" Servantem ripas alta non vidit in herba."

If he speaks of Dido, who suffers her hair to play in the wind, he says she had permitted her head of hair to be spread in the air :

" Dederatque comas diffundere vento."

The orators took other liberties, but these were prohibited them. It is not surprising then, that these kinds of composition, wherein such different modes of expression prevailed, and where freedoms and restraints were so very dissimilar, should never have been combined together.

This distinction exists not amongst us. We have no poetical language which differs from that in common use, nor words which take a
different

different fignification in verfe to what they do in profe. The fine paffages of Boffuet, Flechier and Fenelon, of our celebrated orators, are poetry to which nothing is wanting but rhyme; and, on the contrary, many paffages, even in our good poets, are no otherwife diftinguifhable from profe than by the return of the fame found at the end of every couple of lines; and I think no other reafon can be given than what I have juft affigned, for the neceffity under which Corneille, Boileau, and others amongft us, found themfelves, of being fubjected to this return in order to preferve their fuperiority.

However this be, no one has proved better than Mr. Voltaire, that thefe pretended barriers between the two parts of the fame art are eafily broken down: as I obferved before, he has not only treated of the greater part of profe in general, but he has adventured in each particular fpecies of it, in like manner as he has done in every fort of poetry. In the review of his numerous works, let us begin with his romances.

The romance in itfelf is a fort of fhade between poetry and profe; it bears an affinity to the one, by the fhare of imagination contained in it, and to the other by its fimplicity of ftyle. As to plan, it differs little from the epic poem, except in the cataftrophe; but in its digreffions

it

it approaches more nearly to hiftory. A romance is an imaginary hiftory, offered as fabulous; hiftory itfelf is but too often a web of
fables given for truths. In this, perhaps, confifts the moft effential difference between thefe
two fpecies of narrative. In order to diftinguifh them, we muft be previoufly apprifed to
which they belong.

Put into the hands of one unacquainted with
books, the Anecdotes of the Court of Philip
Auguftus and the Memoire de l'Etoile, he will
give equal credit to both; he will fuppofe himfelf, from one of thefe books, made as well acquainted with the affairs of France in the reign
of the father of Louis the Eighth, as he is with
the age of Henry the Fourth by the other.

But if mankind were willing, it would be poffible to eftablifh between thefe two kinds of
writing a much more material difference in their
utility, and render them further diftinguifhable
by their effects. In the firft, the author being
the creator of events, may difpofe them in fuch
a manner, as to deduce from them a wholefome
leffon of morality; in the fecond, having to recite but too often the enormities committed or
conceived by human perverfion, and fupported
by the caprice of fortune, or credited by that
malicious propenfity which gives fuch a rapid

courfe

courfe to calumny, he is unable to offer to his virtuous readers any thing but motives for difcouragement and indignation. A good romance ought to be a reprefentation of the punifhments attending vice; the moft authentic hiftory is feldom other, than a difplay of its triumphs.

It would not then be difficult to prove, that the firft is infinitely preferable to the other, at leaft in point of moral utility. Were it poffible for authors and governments to concur together for the public good, the romance fhould in an efpecial manner be fet apart, to counterbalance, by a defcription of the oppofite virtues, that of thofe vices and enormities the fcandal of which hiftory is doomed to perpetuate. But in every age mankind have read more for amufement, than inftruction. The firft romance writers, like the firft hiftorians, had no other object in view than to pleafe.

The moft ancient productions of this nature with which we are acquainted, are to be found among the Greeks [1], and even thefe are fuffi-

---

[1] I do not here make mention of the hiftory of Job, regarded by a great number of critics as a romance: they hold forth a moral, as falutary and fublime as the ftory in itfelf is pathetic: but the place this work holds in holy writ will not permit us to clafs it among the monuments of fimple literature.

ciently

ciently modern. Complicated and pathetic incidents little allied to probability, and ftill lefs
to morality, conftitute the merit of Theagenes
and Cariclea, of Ifmenes and Ifmenias, both
attributed to bifhops, and of the fmall number
of this kind of compofition which have reached
us, in the language of Homer and Plato.

Among the Romans we perceive none; except
the licentious fatire of Petronius, and the no lefs
licentious and fantaftical metamorphofis of Apu-
lius, are to be reckoned fuch. The firft is generally confidered an allegory, but ought rather
to be looked on as the offspring of an intempe-
rate raving. A low ground-work, infamous digreffions, fome fallies of wit, and a few happy
verfes, compofe the merit of this work: if it
poffeffed any allufions they are loft to us; but it
evidently held up no model of any kind.

As to the Golden Afs, it is probable that without the fable of Pfyche this amplification of a
filthy tale in Lucan would have made as little
noife as the original; and even with this fupple-
ment, can its prefervation be deemed of any great
advantage to the Latin language, while fo many
precious relics of it are loft?

The enlightened ages of antiquity having held
this branch of literature in fmall eftimation, it
developed itfelf with fplendor in the midft of
barbarifm.

barbarifm. About the eleventh century, the tafte for romances was again reftored, but under a form wholly new. The marvellous of every kind was pufhed to the extreme; heroifm and magic acted extravagant parts in them; knights and enchanters became gods rather than men; it is hard to determine whether the prodigies afcribed to the latter, were more abfurd than the atchievements of the former.

This tafte lafted a confiderable time: there was even in this immenfe progeny of folly two diftinct generations, that of Amadis, or the Round Table, and of Charlemagne with his twelve Peers. From thefe two ftocks an inconceivable multitude of chimerical heroes have arifen, in whofe hiftories notwithftanding we often meet with intereft, pleafantry, and even traits of genius which would do credit to modern productions, the prevailing topics of all are greatnefs of foul, generofity, delicacy, and intrepidity, all carried, as I have remarked, to excefs, together with extravagant marks of refpect and fubmiffion to the fair fex.

It is fingular enough that imagination fhould thus aim at exalting human nature, precifely at the period when it was more degraded than at any other time. Affuredly, whatever may be faid, it was nothing lefs than the manners of the

P   times

times which romance writers delineated in their works. It is true that the age believed in forcery, but it was impoffible that it could give credit either to the magnanimity of the knights, or the virtue of their miftreffes. The firft could not but be regarded as tyrants, in whom meannefs and rapacity abounded, ftill more than pride and magnificence. Rendered invulnerable from their armor, whether engaged in the caufe of their country or in private quarrel, they were much more anxious to fecure themfelves, than to attack their adverfaries; and accordingly never were battles lefs bloody than at that period.

In the fame age when fo many marvellous feats were invented to the honor of prowefs, it was that chivalry was moft unfortunate, the worft conducted, and moft humiliated : it was after thofe extravagant crufades, in which the flower of the European nobility had, for two fucceffive centuries, delivered themfelves up to be flaughtered by the fcum of the Afiatic populace; in which our heroes had found means to be conftantly beaten by bafe Egyptians and effeminate Syrians, unaccuftomed to oppofe any other enemy.

The chaftity of the women of thofe days kept pace with the valor of the heroes. In thefe pompous tales, female modefty is more frequently com-

compounded for than reverenced; every other record of the times prove that debauchery and licentioufnefs were at leaft as prevalent then, as in ages which are called more corrupt, but which are only more polite; they poffeffed at leaft no more than a veil, which correfponded with the decency of the latter in concealing its deformity. The romances of chivalry are then, without exception, chimeras of the brain, and in no refpect portraits of the times.

This tafte prevailed 'till the revival of letters, and was confined to France and Spain; the Italians, among whom it does not appear to have been till then adopted, now gave into it in their turn with a fort of fury, but they caufed it to affume a more agreeable drefs. They conceived the idea of clothing it in verfe, and embellifhing by new fictions thofe which the French and Spaniards had already multiplied in a coarfe profe. Pulci, Bayardo, Ariofto, and Taffo, diftinguifhed themfelves in this new walk, and infinitely furpaffed their models.

What appears again extraordinary, is that the Spaniards, with whofe genius thefe illufions feemed moft congenial, and among whom they had in fact abounded for feveral ages, became difgufted with them precifely at the time that they appear to have been adopted by the Italians The ingenious

P 2   Cervantes

Cervantes ufed the fame art to effect their overthrow, to which they were indebted for their rife:
his Don Quixote poffeffed the double and very
uncommon merit of being at the fame time an
excellent parody and an interefting work in itfelf,
independent of the criticifm it contained.

The Amadis and the Giants were now fucceeded in the Spanifh literature by fhorter tales,
brought nearer to ordinary life. The imagination difplayed in thefe was lefs extravagant and
wild; the antient Moorifh gallantry was blended
with a more rational heroifm. This was de-
nominated a novel; and Cervantes, the deftroyer
of the ancient fpecies, deferves to be placed at
the head of the new.

France had no part in this reformation; the
fury of theological difputes, and the political
feuds which fucceeded them, feemed to abforb
the active power of mens minds. Rabelais is
almoft the only author of thefe times we can
quote who gave a loofe to his imagination: but
what a ftyle of writing, and what an imagination
were his!

I admire the good fortune of thofe who un-
derftand him, and can find delight in his works,
but I envy them not. All I think wonderful in
this ftrange jumble of obfcenity and erudition,
folly and burlefque on every thing held facred,

is

is its fuccefs. Whilft wretches were throughout all France committed to the flames for receiving the facrament in both kinds, and with leavened bread, who acknowledged the Bible for their rule of faith; at the fide of this very Bible was placed a work, which, like it, was called the *Book* by way of eminence, containing a collection of difgufting obfcenities, in which the Old and New Teftaments, the church, her minifters and facraments, and more efpecially the eucharift, that grand object of religious controverfy, was turned into derifion with a freedom and groffnefs fcarcely to be equalled in the fatires of Luther. and Calvin.

When at length thefe commotions had fome-what fubfided, and the minds of men, appeafed by the latter years of the reign of Henry the Fourth, had begun to benefit by an intercourfe with the Italians, and ftill more with the Spa-niards, fo long their conquerors, a revolution took place, equally important to the literature of France, as that effected by the piaftres of the new world was to the circumftances of mankind. The credit of this is afcribed to Cardinal Rich-lieu, who moft affuredly in no way contributed to it: it was in embryo, and even ripening into birth, long before his time. Neither Malherbe, Durfe, Gombreville, or any of thofe whofe talents

P 3

he

he afterwards feemed to have in pay, had been encouraged by him; almoft all thefe being born with the age in which they lived, had already cultivated and exercifed their genius before a minifter appeared about the throne who feemed to hold either them or their works in eftimation.

Befides, this minifter in his conduct difcovered himfelf rather the enemy of tafte than its patron; he interefted himfelf in the Cid but to oppofe it, to difcredit, to afflict and to diftrefs the author; he repulfed Mainard with harfhnefs. The inftitution of the French Academy is rather a proof of his defpotifm, than of an enlightened tafte for letters. His only view in forming this felect committee was to infure to himfelf panegyric, not to perfect literature. Corneille was not admitted till very late, after having experienced more than one refufal, in fpite of his poetical renown. Boileau, La Fontaine, Racine, would probably have been excluded, had providence fo long protracted his life and his power, or, like Corneille, they muft have purchafed their admiffion by their meannefs *.

* After experiencing two refufals, he found himfelf oppofed to a man called Balefdens, who would have gained his point had he not had more modefty than the company. See on this fubject the 4th vol. of thefe Annals, page 408.

What-

Whatever agent Louis the Thirteenth had made choice of at the time when he took the bifhop of Lucon into his councils, all the genius which preceded the age of Louis the Fourteenth would have equally fhone forth; tafte and letters would have been no way impeded in their progreffion, which was not retarded by the indifference of cardinal Mazarine, or accelerated by the zeal of his predeceffor.

However this be, the dawn of good tafte which began to appear, fecured Gombreville, Calprenede, and Scuderi, from that outrageous difregard to good fenfe which had given birth to Amadis and Efplandian. They bid adieu to fairies and witches; their heroes were lefs marvellous, their heroines more decent; they feemed nearer on a level with the reader, though the grandeur of the one, and the virtue of the other, were ftill far fuperior to human nature, and to the ordinary intercourfe of life.

Perhaps it may be allowable to regret this age of romancery, if we may hazard the term. In my opinion, the authors of Cleopatra, Caffandra, Cyrus, and Clelia, have been very unjuftly accufed of transforming the principal characters of antiquity into people of ordinary rank. Nothing is more ill founded than this criticifm. In thefe productions love is ennobled, and always pre-

fents

sents itself under a respectable form, valor, magnanimity, delicacy, modesty, every virtue which
can adorn the two sexes are here described, with
a splendor which at once excites admiration and
attachment.

La Carte de Tendre, l'Echo d'Horatius
Cocles, les Enigmes de Brutus, de Lucrece,
may have furnished matter for epigrams; the
length of the works, and that of the metaphysi-
cal dissertations they contain, may tire; a certain
affectation of displaying a genteel style, of shew-
ing a familiarity with the language of the court,
may displease; but where is the mental labor
that is faultless? Lastly, many of these stains are
confined to Clelia, the Echo, the Carte Tendre,
and the Enigmas: we meet with nothing of this
kind in Pharamond or Cleopatra; and even
those three insipidities, so cruelly exposed by
Boileau, do not offend in the passages where
they are placed, such is the address with which
they are employed, so skilfully is their weaknefs
concealed from view, and such is the noblenefs,
grandeur, and heroism of the remaining part.

What citizens are the father and mother of
Clelia, or Arons, or Amilcar? Were that epithet applicable to them becaufe the ground of
their adventures resemble the ordinary distresses
of life? This is a further injuftice. What is it
then, we may ask, which furnifhes the subject
for

for poems and tragedies, if it be not the effect of paffions alike difcoverable in the Rue de St. Denis, in the Strand, in the Calle del Sol, as at Verfailles, St. James's, or St. Idelphonfo?

This at leaft cannot be denied, that thefe romances, at the prefent day configned to oblivion, or the perufal of fome amateurs or plagiarifts, who have had recourfe to them for ideas which their own barrennefs of invention could not fupply them with, are prodigies of imagination, refource, fecundity, and art, and, perhaps, the fineft models it is poffible to lay before mankind to difpofe them to virtue.

Let it be obferved too, that thofe precepts of courage and magnanimity which the authors inculcated through their heroes, were practifed by themfelves. The men of genius of thofe days diftinguifhed themfelves no lefs by their courage, than their imagination. Calprenede, when told that the mitred monarch of France thought his verfes bafe, retorted this infult by a fally which could never have efcaped a man of doubtful valor.

The bravery of Cyrano was extended even to rafhnefs; a moft valuable anecdote is preferved of him. Two of his friends were engaged in a quarrel, furrounded by thirty men, who attacked them fword in hand; Cyrano perceives them

from

from a window, rushes on the aggressors, difperses them, and carries off his friends in triumph. No romance has suppofed any adventure fo incredible and fo fortunate.

The memory of Scudery, amongft us devoted to ridicule, ought in every virtuous and enlightened mind to be confecrated to refpect. He had dedicated to queen Chriftina his poem of Alaric, wherein he had inferted an eulogium on the count de la Gardie, then the favorite minifter of that princefs; this is the cuftom of poets in every age: but what follows is not the cuftom of any. The minifter was difgraced; Chriftina required Scudery to retrench his praifes in a new edition of the poem; fhe intimated to him a prefent of ten thoufand livres Tournois of that day, which were worth more than twenty of the prefent. Scudery was not rich: he anfwered, " that no reward fhould induce him to " deftroy the altar at which he had facrificed." Chriftina ought to have repaid this refufal better than a compliance; fhe kept her money; fhe was a philofopher, and Scudery was not. It fhould appear that fuch men ought to be pardoned in drawing their heroes thus haughty and generous.

When cuftom had introduced fatiety in this new fpecies, and a change of tafte, the fruit ot incon-

inconftancy rather than of perfection, had brought
it into difrepute, Mad. de la Fayetts, or Segrais
under her name, and afterwards Mad. de Ville-
dieu, Mad. de Gomes, and a thoufand others,
difplayed another fpecies of compofition, the
merit of which was ftill due to the Spaniards:
I mean that of hiftorical novels. Thefe were
miniatures of thofe Coloffufes of which I have
been fpeaking.

They likewife took names known in hiftory,
to which they adapted fictions fhorter, more pathetic, and more fimilar to thofe which occur
daily, or of a different fort of fingularity than
the grand martial atchievements and exemplary
chaftity of Oroondates, Candace, &c. but ftill
thefe tales, which interefted the heart without
alarming modefty, were poffeffed of delicacy,
imagination, and beauty.

This tafte prevailed till that vile inundation
of obfcenity which has poifoned literature, the
Sophas, Tanzai, Angola, &c. difgufting caricatures, wherein, to the difgrace of our age, its
manners are but too faithfully delineated, and
in which the romance, till then employed in
elevating the mind, melting the heart, or at leaft
in furnifhing matter for amufement, ferves only
to vilify human nature, and to prove, as well as
to perpetuate, its degeneracy.

Mr.

Mr. Voltaire, who in his Pucelle but too closely followed the fashion of the times, has guarded against it in his romances; he has opened to himself a way absolutely new. He has neither taken the mad sublimity of Amadis, nor the heroism, too exalted for our comprehension, of Oroondates, the pathetic simplicity of the Princess of Cleves, or the degrading burlesque of the Mazulhim, &c. He has chalked out to himself a path, in which an enlightened philosophy beams forth; a criticism almost always useful, and, with some few exceptions, a chearful gaiety, in which every one may honorably partake.

In the romances of his best time, as in his tragedies, the outline of each is varied; Zadig is soft, agreeable, and creates a smile in the mind. Though several chapters are taken from Ariosto, or the Chinese Tales inserted at the end of Du Halde's collection, or from the Arabian Nights Entertainment; and though it contains no very splendid adventures, and that the interest is not lively, it is notwithstanding so well written, so replete with wit, with truth, and satisfactory representations, that it is read with a pleasure always new.

Candidus offers the most melancholy subject concealed under the most humorous garb, with
that

that laughing philofophy peculiar to Mr. Voltaire, and which I repeat it fhould feem to have given him an excellent comic genius, he turns into complete ridicule the system of " whatever " is, is right," maintained by fo many philofophers, and caufes a thoufand burfts of laughter in his readers, in placing before them in every page, and with a mafterly pencil, the evils infeparable from fociety.

There is more imagination in this fecond romance than in Zadig; the fcene of the fix kings dining together at Venice, is, in my opinion, an eminent production of genius, as well in itfelf as from the manner in which it is defcribed, and the ferious reflections it has a tendency to produce. Some few paffages excepted, fuch as a certain *genealogy*, a groffnefs which but ill agrees with the beauty of the remaining part, Candidus feems to me the *chef d'œuvre* of fterling ridicule, of elegance, and, what is of more importance, of real philofophy, at leaft of fuch as can be introduced into a tale.

L'Ingenu again is in another ftyle, and perhaps the moft perfect of the three. It is to be regretted that fome friend of the author did not perfuade him to expunge fome wretched puns, or indecent buffooneries which difgrace it. He prefents to us pathetic pictures, all

taken

taken from common life and daily occurrences, without even excepting the Baſtile.

It may be remarked, that it is the only one of Mr. Voltaire's proſe writings, as Tancred is the ſole tragedy, in which he has attempted to paint a ſcene really pathetic. The adventure of Mad. de St. Ives, her illneſs and her death, force tears from us. One would have been tempted to believe that Mr. Voltaire was deſirous in this piece of entering the liſts againſt the cataſtrophe of the new Heloiſe itſelf, imitated in the Engliſh Clariſſa; but it is another ſtyle; it is even ſo different, that we cannot compare them: I have already remarked, Mr. Voltaire did not poſſeſs this ſpecies of excellence.

After theſe two romances, his Scarmentado, his Micromegas, and his Memnon, will be always read with pleaſure. Too ſtrong perſonalities and indecencies, too thinly veiled, detract from his Candidus and ſeveral others, the produce of his old age, that is to ſay, when years and his great habit of writing rendered him leſs difficult in his ſtyle, and his great certainty of being read made him leſs delicate in his expreſſions.

O F

OF THE

HISTORICAL WORKS

OF

Mr. VOLTAIRE.

HISTORICAL WORKS,

OF

MR. VOLTAIRE.

AFTER thus traverſing with ſo much ſucceſs thoſe departments of literature which
depend on the imagination, Mr. Voltaire adventured into that of hiſtory, wherein this
faculty of the mind is oftentimes more dangerous
than uſeful. Is this attempt to be regarded in
him as a temerity?—Although on this head
there may be ſome uncertainty in the ſuffrages,
it appears that the opinion of the diſintereſted
is fixed and unanimous, in conſidering the hiſto-
rical productions of Mr. Voltaire, as one of the
titles which beſt juſtify his fame.

Q

I ſpeak

I fpeak not of the Hiftory of Charles the XIIth, a piece worthy of the reception it has met with; interefting, and finely written; but wherein the fingularity of the events is more remarkable than the ftyle.   This work is written with wifdom, dignity, and elegance, but not in fuch a manner as to take from a rival the hope of equaling it.

What feems to leave no room for competition, what infures to Mr. Voltaire not only a dif-tinguifhed, but fuperior rank to all hiftorians, either modern or even of antiquity; what gives us authority to regard him as the creator of a new fpecies in this department, ftill more than in that of the theatre or of romance, is his Age of Louis the XIVth.

This work, on its firft appearance, excited univerfal admiration — even envy herfelf was ftruck dumb—fhe has fince recovered her fpeech, but to charge the author with fome trifling in-accuracies, many of which even, were the faults of workmen and copyifts.   But there is but one concurring voice on the beauty of its frontifpiece, on the portrait of the political ftate of Europe which it exhibits at the commencement of this celebrated reign; a fort of portrait with which both ancients and moderns were alike unacquainted,

and

and which feemed even at its birth, to poffefs its full maturity of perfection.

The chapters on thofe ridiculous contefts of the *fronde*, which would have entailed equal mifery and contem t on the kingdom, had not forty fucceeding years of fplendor done away its infamy, were received with little lefs avidity ; and in thofe too of which the arts, the government, of Louis the XIVth or his views, are the fubject ; his projects and meafures are at once delineated with fo much art and dignity, that the very errors of his adminiftration feem to confirm the refpect his real qualities are calculated to infpire.

His abridged Narrative of Ecclefiaft cal Quarrels was received with equal gratification : of thofe contefts but too much multiplied in an age wherein the progrefs of letters ought to have made them lefs frequent. Mankind had never yet beheld an example of fuch clearnefs in the expofition of the caufes whence thefe diffentions arofe, a like impartiality in the relation of facts, fuch a grandeur pervading throughout a narrative : a dignity, accompanied with fo adroit a trifling, as ferved but to develope truth, and almoft to render reafoning fuperfluous. Did we poffefs fuch a monument of Grecian or Roman antiquity, it would be reverenced amongft us even to idolatry.

Q 2   If

If the body of the hiftory, that is to fay, the fummary of political events, has appeared fomewhat inferior, it is perhaps becaufe it is caft into a fhade by thofe brilliant paffages which precede and follow it; and further, becaufe an abridgement, with whatever fkill it be defigned, has always fomething dry in itfelf; hiftory, properly fo called, is fupported by digreffions, in a ftill greater degree than by reflections.

Criticifm has found in his Effay on Univerfal Hiftory, a greater fund of refource and fupport. It cannot be diffembled that this work is the fruit of that emulation which Mr. Voltaire felt to contend in every department of literature againft thofe writers whofe names are enrolled in the lifts of immortality. The famous Treatife of Boffuet on Univerfal Hiftory was the object of his rivalfhip, perhaps of his jealoufy: hence has refulted to literature a production of a nature wholly different. Mr. Voltaire, in afpiring to walk by the fide of Boffuet, has abfolutely run counter to the plan chalked out by that eloquent prelate.

Much lefs did he propofe to himfelf the fame end, or rather it fhould feem, that as he has been reproached, it was a direct contrary one he had in view. Boffuet wrote but to fhew the relation which every grand event of ancient hiftory had

with

with the eftablifhment of Chriftianity, and confequently to ftrengthen the refpect due to that
religion. Mr. Voltaire, it muft be acknowledged,
feems to have laborioufly fought to lay before us
in his Portrait of Modern Hiftory, all the greater
and lefs events beft calculated to do away that
refpect. Boffuet leads all to faith, and Mr.
Voltaire all to infidelity.

I fhall fhortly give my opinion on that philofophy which tranfpires through almoft all his
works; but befoie we pafs on to this fubject, I
cannot forbear faying a word on one of the moft
unjuft criticifms this writer has experienced.
Five years after his death a work appeared, the
principal object of which was to abufe him, particularly on the fubject of his hiftorical productions; he is in every page of it quoted as an
hiftorian, and never without infult. If we are
to credit Mr. l'Abbé de Mably, " He has
" finifhed all his works, before he well knew
" what he was about to fay ; he deals out falli-
" neffes with emphafis: he cannot fee as far as
" his nofe; he is the moft frivolous and enter-
" taining of all hiftorians; in his Charles the
" XIIth. he runs like a fool after a fool, his
" Univerfal Hiftory is but a pafquinade, &c. &c."

Thefe ftrange expreffions difcover in the critic
a very blind prejudice, and a moft unjuft ani-

Q 3   mofity.

mofity.   Not only Mr. Voltaire is neither frivolous
nor trifling in his hiftorical compofitions ; but
the reproach he moft juftly lies open to, is that
of being too ferious and too fentimental ; that
of exacting from his readers a too conftant attention, and of prefenting every moment deductions
which, to minds not familiarized with habits of
reflection, muft render it fatiguing to follow
him.

It is even a very ftriking fingularity, that the
man who is every where elfe fo light and gay,
fhould be capable of fuch gravity and unre-
mitting labour.   Far from being playful and
frivolous, he difcovers himfelf ferious even
to coldnefs, and auftere to drynefs.   When he
allows himfelf any malignant allufions, the humour is in the things, or the arrangement of the
facts, and very rarely in the words themfelves.

The Abbè de Mably ought to have been the
laft who fhould have hazarded this cenfure ; he,
who has attempted at humour, as far as he was
able, in a work with the nature of which it was ftill
lefs compatible ; who in a collection of dogma-
tical precepts, fays, " that Janfenifm would again
" kindle a civil flame at the beards of the phi-
" lofophers and their difciples, if, &c." which,
to men of tafte, will not appear a very refined
ftroke of humour ; who fomewhere elfe fays,
that

that " an hiftorian ought, in policy, to be fome-
" what more fkilful than his hero;" which will
appear rather an oddity than a jeft.

He further reproaches Mr. Voltaire with fome
voluntary fcepticifms, and is defirous that hiftory fhould be in fome fort an epic poem.

PART

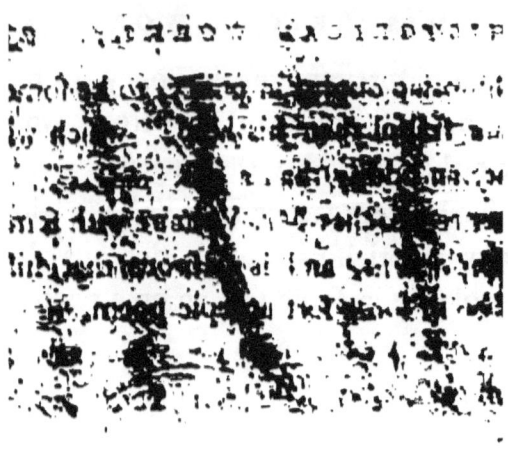

PART the THIRD.

OF THE

PHILOSOPHY

OF

Mr. VOLTAIRE,

AND HIS

WORKS on RELIGION.

PHILOSOPHY

OF

MR. VOLTAIRE,

AND HIS

WORKS ON RELIGION.

WE are at length arrived at that path, which, of all thofe that ferved to conduct this furprifing man to fame, was the one in which he feemed moft emulous of diftinguifhing himfelf; that, in which he delighted to walk during his whole life, and to which, if we may ufe the term, his excurfions into every other were rendered fubfervient. Philofophy was his idol, his paffion; and by this term he underftood a hatred to what he called prejudices, a boldnefs in combating received opinions of every kind, but more efpecially on matters of religion.

His manner of treating thefe important fubjects, has, as I have obferved on the occafion of

one

one of his Epic Poems, gained him the fuffrages of the youthful part of his readers, ftill
more moderate in their encomiums than their
invectives; thofe of women, inconfiderate, and
too eafily feduced by what pleafes them, to be
capable of withftanding thofe *bon mots* which
are fubftituted for arguments; thofe of the greater
part of men of the world, feldom well informed, and ftill more rarely capable of reflection, and who always giving the fafhion to,
or receiving it from the women, were naturally led to unite with them in their efteem for
a man, who could make them laugh while dif-
cuffing the moft ferious fubjects.

On the other hand, the devotees of both
fexes, ferious men, who regarded religion as the
fafeguard of manners and the public tranquility;
the clergy, whofe office it is to inculcate the
duties of religion, and who naturally perfuade
themfelves it is their duty to defend it: have
conceived a reafonable horror againft a man
who openly declared himfelf its enemy. They
profcribed him as a public corruptor, who was
fo much the more dangerous, as his poifons
were, as they faid, adminiftred in the form of
remedies—he pretended an ardent love of truth,
only to gain the more credit for his errors,
and further, becaufe whilft multiplying blafphemies,

phemies, he covered them with an appearance
fo fpecious, with a levity fo well adapted to feduce, that he enfured almoft as many accom-
plices as readers.

Between thefe two decifions, fo different, he
who would wifh to form an impartial opinion,
muft be compelled to incline towards the more
fevere.   The admiration he cannot refufe to the
talents of the writer, is diminifhed when he
enquires what good has been done by the philofopher.

Not but that in the latter character Mr. Voltaire has been of very great benefit to mankind.
Being of all men who have written the moft
univerfally read, who even to the higheft point
of perfection poffeffed the art of expreffing his
ideas with perfpicuity, and of infinuating them
with art, he has made an infinite number of
profelytes, and he ought to have his due tribute
of thanks, when his notions have been found to
conduce to the public welfare and the general
benefit of fociety.   Of thefe he poffeffes many,
on literature, education, government, legiflation, and even on jurifprudence.

Though he did not immediately work a reformation, becaufe he did not poffefs the requifite power, he kindled that general fpirit, which
in time produces it, and therein effected a real
change.

change. Manners are become more polifhed, if not more pure, and the eyes of men are more open to what may do them harm. Decrees, which thirty years earlier would not have excited the leaft alarm, have been annulled by the voice of the people, which has compelled their governors to yield to the claims of reafon and juftice. Debates, partly political and partly religious, which at the commencement of the prefent century, and perhaps ftill later, would have led to violence and perfecution, have excited no intereft whatever. The general indifference has rendered them lefs acute, and their effects lefs tedious and mifchievous; and perhaps, in the end, may in time wholly prevent them, and thus fpare our children from a fcourge which has afflicted and difgraced their anceftors.

Juftice obliges us to acknowledge, that it is in a great meafure to Mr. Voltaire we are indebted for thefe benefits. So far he is entitled to claim the gratitude of his contemporaries and of pofterity. I will even go further—had he confined himfelf, in treating on religion, to fhew how far, under pretence of enforcing its privileges, the fpirit of its founder has been departed from—to what a degree, paffion has fometimes prevailed over morality—if, in a mafterly

defcription

defcription of the crimes produced by fanati-
· cifm, the fcandals of fuperftition, the meannefs
of avarice—veiled under a venerable form, addreffing mankind he had faid, " Thefe horrors
" are no lefs oppofite to true religion than to
" reafon;" an idea fo well expreffed in Alzira,

" Our God is their's, my fon, but they infult him."

If even he had fometimes embellifhed thefe ferious
truths by the graces of his ftyle, and made ufe
of his powers of ridicule to expofe the oppofite
errors; he had ftill merited the title of a bene-
factor to mankind.

Unfortunately, he has not confined himfelf
within thefe limits. His defign feems not to
have been to prune the tree, but to tear it up
by the roots. In his latter years efpecially, he
feems to have imbibed an anti-religious fanaticifm, more outrageous than that of which he
accufes the priefts, who were the object of
that by which he himfelf was actuated. Affuredly no enthufiaft of any fect, or of any
reformation, has allowed himfelf in fuch violent
and cruel invectives againft infidelity, as he has
multiplied out of number againft chriftianity.
His hatred of this religion was become an univerfal, a real mania, it took poffeffion of all his   ·

4   faculties,

faculties, fpreading diforder through them, and leading him often to offend equally againft the laws of logic, as thofe of decency. I fhall here quote but one inftance, drawn from his drama, but from a piece wherein he was more occupied by philofophy than poetry.

It is the character of Joad in Olympia, and that of the priefthood in general, whom he ftrived to render odious : that factious, intriguing, and defpotic fpirit, which he attributes to the chriftian clergy, he wifhed to defcribe and vilify, in delineating the character of a pontiff exempt from all thefe vices. In order that we may not miftake his intentions, he has taken care to explain them himfelf in the remarks which follow the piece.

He there fays in direct terms, " By what right " does Joad the prieft arm his Levites againft " a queen to whom he has taken an oath of alle- " giance? By what right does he caufe her to be " murdered in her old age ? Was it for Joad to " confpire againft, and kill her ? He was her " fubject, and affuredly, confiftent with our " manners and laws, it was no more allowable " in Joad to caufe his queen to be affaffinated, " than it would have been in an archbifhop of " Canterbury to have put queen Elizabeth to
" death,

" death, becaufe fhe had condemned Mary
" Stuart."

Certainly, the comparifon is as unjuft, as the
reafoning is incorrect. How does Joad become
the fubject of Athalia ? How is fhe his queen ?
She was an alien, an ufurper; fhe enjoyed the
throne, it is true, but fhe had paved her
way thither by the flaughter of all whofe birth
gave them a title to it. How is Mr. Voltaire
authorifed in faying that Joad had fworn alle-
giance to her ? If even from motives of policy
he had confented to pay her that homage, would
that alone have been fufficient to juftify us in
applying the terms of rebellion and affaffination
to a revolution directed by him who recalled the
lawful heir to the crown, preferved through his
means ?

Let us fuppofe that Catharine of Medicis had
caufed Henry the Third to be murdered, and
had poffeffed herfelf of the crown of France,
as Athalia did that of Jerufalem; that Henry
the Fourth at this epocha had been a child; that
an archbifhop of Paris had found means to con-
vey him out of the hands of thofe who by murder and poifon confpired his death; and that
when this prince came of age, he had prefented
him to the people; that a revolt had in confequence taken place, wherein the ufurper was

R   deftroyed:

deſtroyed: could this prelate have been accuſed of conſpiring againſt, and aſſaſſinating his ſovereign?

Examples of this ſort of injuſtice, and theſe wanderings in Mr. Voltaire, are many in his philoſophical works. He ſomewhere ſays,

" I have done more in my time than Luther and Calvin."

This is true in every ſenſe, but more eſpecially inaſmuch as thoſe celebrated reformers ſought only to repair the building; they did not pull it down; they lopped off thoſe exuberances by which, in their opinion, the purity of the Chriſtian doctrines had been ſullied: but they revered the foundation of the ſtructure; and when even the ties which united them with the Catholics were torn aſunder, they ſtill retained the goſpel as the guide of their faith and conduct. But in the reformation of Mr. Voltaire, what remains to encourage the weak, to conſole the wretched, to curb the wicked, and to ſerve as a ſign of union to all men?

" Deiſm, ſays Mr. Voltaire, the idea of a God, the diſpenſer of future rewards and puniſhments, has been the religion of great geniuſes in every age: it was that of Julian, of Marcus Aurelius, Cicero, Scipio, and others. Why, poſſeſſing as much underſtanding as Cicero, ſhould I hold

I   the

the religion of my times in more refpect than he did that of his? His philofophic works are complete courfes of incredulity, and they are reprinted *ad ufum Delphini.* Why fhould I be thought culpable for a conduct thus honorably rewarded in him?

" Your cenfure of my pretended bo'dnefs is but a continuation of your inconfiftency. In attacking your belief I cannot do more harm, than he who declares aloud that he doubts of every thing; the toleration of every age towards his fcepticifm, fufficiently proves this virtue to be no way detrimental. Why not extend it then to me?"

This is nearly the fummary of what Mr. Voltaire has urged in defence of his anti-chriftian effufions. I have long fince expreffed my fentiments on the fubject—leaving the fyftem to thofe whofe province it is to inculcate, and to defend it; I never confidered its doctrines but in a political point of view. It is not in the character of a miffionary, but a philofopher, that I fhall reply to Mr. Voltaire in the following terms:

Your idea of toleration is a fallacious one, and you rely on the example of Cicero for your fupport in it, with little reafon; circumftances, which alter every thing, are materially different

R 2

in

in the eighteenth, from what they were in the firſt century of our æra.

1ſt. In that orator's time, not only the body of the people, but even the higher claſſes of the citizens, did not read at all. The exceſſive price of books, and the difficulty of procuring them even for money, rendered them an · objeĉt of luxury, and confequently an appendage to opulence. Thus all the opinions debated in the ſchools, or in writings, reached thoſe only who had leiſure and time to ſpare in attending theſe philoſophical diſcuſſions, or men of fortune, who amuſed themſelves with them in their cloſets, which even at Rome ſcarcely compoſed, in that age, one millionth part of the nation.

2dly. Cicero treated theſe ſubjeĉts philoſophically; his ſtyle was adapted to the gravity of his matter. If he imitated Plato in the familiar turn ·of his dialogue, he kept him no leſs in view, in the ſeverity with which he avoided whatever had a tendency to ridicule. He allowed himſelf no other embelliſhments than perſpicuity and elegance: a further reaſon to confirm us in the opinion, that he ſought for readers only in a very confined order of ſociety.

3dly. Whatever impreſſion the opinions of Cicero might make on this ſmall body of readers, or even granting that their number was more

con-

confiderable, no material evil could flow from
it, fince paganifm, whofe divinities he queftioned, had no dogmas.   It confifted in ceremonies
and rites, indifferent enough in themfelves, and
in fupport of which it was no way to be apprehended that any one fhould become inflamed,
fince the policy of the ftate had ceafed to confider them among the principal engines of government.

On the other hand, the very mythology whofe
chimeras he divefted of reverence, neither offered fuch precepts of wifdom or examples of
virtue, as to caufe the philofophy which brought
them into difrepute to be any way deemed dangerous.   Affuredly fuch principles of refined
morality, regulated by reafon and a love of the
public welfare, as are difplayed in the Offices,
&c. would bear to be put in competition as to
the benefits likely to accrue to fociety from the
effects of each, with the ftory of Mercury the
god of thieves, or that of Vulcan's nets.   The
general order of fociety could fuftain no injury
by the contempt into which altars had fallen dedicated to a patron of robbers, or ferving as
examples of conjugal infidelity.

4thly. With regard to the indulgence in which
his philofophical reafonings are held at the prefent day, as to the ufe made of them without

R 3   fcruple

scruple and without alarm in our schools, and the little concern with which we behold them in the hands of every description of readers, the inconsistency you point out in such a conduct will not justify you. Custom, the difference of our idioms, the title of an ancient, the veneration he inspires, might all be urged in excuse for the negligence of tutors and governments; but, in fact, they are not justly liable to any reproach on this head. The truth of the divinities, and the religion of the times in which he lived, are the objects of the Roman orator's enquiry; the dreams of paganism, which he treats as puerile illusions. These deities, and this system, are now no more. It is not to be apprehended that the reflections of a heathen philosopher on the sacred fowls, or the adventures of Jupiter, will cause any doubts in the mind of a reader on the mysteries of the Christian religion. We may safely put them into the hands of a pupil, as models of purity in a language he is studying, without being any way apprehensive of their making impressions capable of changing his belief.

But can you avail yourself of any of these pleas? Are the times the same? Does our system, our religious principles or our doctrines resemble those fables which Cicero derided?

Will

Will the fubject, the tendency, and the fpirit
of your works bear a comparifon with thofe of
Cicero in any of thefe refpects? Your object
in writing, efpecially on religion, was to be
read by men of all ages and conditions. The
numberlefs pleafantries with which your works
on this fubject abound, could have no other end.
The very form of thefe pamphlets, always fhort,
and confequently eafily procured, convenient to
be read or retained, and moreover within the reach
of every inquifitive perfon, is an index which
reveals your fecret. It is then the multitude,
the body of the people, you were defirous of fe-
ducing, or, if you pleafe, of perfuading: now
what good end could you propofe to yourfelf or
to the world in doing this?

I gave you due praife for having held up the
quarrels of the Janfenifts to ridicule; for rendering odious the perfecution of the Proteftants
of the laft century: doubtlefs, a pertinacity in
requiring of the Janfenifts a retraction in itfelf
immaterial, was altogether as extravagant as their
obftinacy in refufing it; the expulfion of the
Proteftants, or at leaft the conditions on which
alone they were allowed the right of breathing their
native air, was cruel. You did right in expofing
to the derifion or abhorrence of the public; thefe
two effects of folly and defpotifm; but is it the

R 4   fame

fame with your infulting farcafms and endlefs jokes at the expence of whatever Chriftianity holds up as facred to the people.

You are continually laying claim to the privilege of toleration, for which I am no lefs an advocate than yourfelf; but you make it to confift in rights which moft affuredly, could never belong to it. Toleration extends no farther than in leaving free from reftraint the opinions and even the conduct of men, fo far as they do not interfere with the public welfare; in leaving every one at liberty in matters that relate merely to himfelf to act agreeably to his own confcience and opinion; but not in permitting him to labor at altering, or in allowing to affume a controul over thofe of others.

Thus, whether you comply with the external forms of religion or not, as long as you confine yourfelf to a filent omiffion merely, I think that the police has not even a right to take cognizance of it. In refufing to yourfelf the advantage of thefe falutary obfervances, you endanger your own foul only; the magiftrate and the paftor can do no more than exhort, and lament for you; whilft peaceably permitting you thus to eftrange yourfelf from your religious duty, they fulfil theirs, they are tolerant.

But

But if you render thefe ordinances ridiculous to your neighbours; if you infpire them with contempt for the myfteries which are celebrated in them, you then become a teacher; you difturb good order; you are then intolerant yourfelf, fince you endeavour to deftroy the faith of thofe who paffed over your incredulity. From that moment you are criminal, and, unlefs you are repreffed, may do confiderable harm.

Were you to go about to infult a monarch in his palace, to proclaim aloud that it is folly to folicit favors of him, or to hold his minifters in refpect, to brave him in the prefence of his courtiers—where is the captain of his guard, or the private fentry, where the meanneft of his officers, who would not haften to avenge him? What fpectator, though more philofophic than Julian or Cicero, who would dare to blame them? And if, in the fervency of a real or political zeal, they were to ufe you ill, would you have any juft title to complain of oppreffion and tyranny?

You wifh to deftroy the priefthood—you wifh to have foldiers and magiftrates only—but when the fovereign, hurried on by his paffions, fhall have violated the laws; when, like David, he fhall have murdered the hufband to make his wife a widow and to marry her—when, like

Theodofius,

Theodofius, he fhall have profcribed and delivered over a whole people to flaughter, met together to be entertained by your theatric talents—is it on the gentlemen of the long robe we are to rely to arreft his arm, and compel him to deplore his crime? or muft we refort to heroes like Joab, to impofe a penance on him, and compel him to commemorate his forrow by public acts of contrition?

It was an ecclefiaftic who was commiffioned from God to fay to the father of Solomon, *Thou baft finned*. When the Theffalonic maffacre was perpetrated, we may fuppofe that the Roman empire had within it numbers of virtuous lawyers and General officers poffeffed of generofity—thefe ferved, however, but as approvers and minifters to the daftardly cruelty of the prince; had it not been for the heroic courage of a prieft, it had paffed unpunifhed.

What punifhment, fay you, what reparation for the murder of feven thoufand people, to be obliged to abftain for fome months from going to mafs? Doubtlefs the crime was great, and the chaftifement trifling. But had St. Ambrofe adopted a more rigorous one, you would have accufed him of defpotifm and rebellion. It was of lefs importance to expiate the fault already committed, than to prevent the commiffion of a

new

new one: the prince was to be punished, not
degraded; the object was to confine him, without enraging him, to insure the lives of his subjects, without irritating the minds of their go-
vernor. The conduct of St. Ambrose appears
to me a master-piece of religious rigor, and political indulgence.

Let us be cautious of breaking down these
barriers, the only security to miserable subjects
against those monsters who descend to crouch
around the throne, but to acquire a right to devour
the people. It is certainly immaterial to the
public tranquility, whether twenty or an hundred
philosophers deliberate, concur, or perplex one
another, provided their systems, either true or
false, stop here: but it is not a matter of indifference that their freethinking should extend to
the people, who stand in need of guides, or to
their governors, for whom restraint is needful;
which restraint can consist only in the com-
mands of a God, superior even to monarchs
themselves.—A God who speaks; and ministers
who announce his will, appear then to be necef-
ary. These will abuse their power—that may be
—but would there not be still greater danger in
unbounded licence? The only means of prevent-
ing this, is that of rendering the clergy virtuous,
and that the interest of its members will prompt
them

them to be.　In an enlightened age, the efficacy of their remonftrances depends more efpecially on the refpeêt they infpire as a body of men; a temporizing prieft is, of all others, the bafeft and moft defpicable of mankind.　Had not St. Ambrofe been a prelate of irreproachable chaæter, the courtiers would have derided his refiftance, or he would not have dared to make any.

Since then, except in an age of barbarifm, the power. of the clergy can never be held in fuch refpeêt as to become formidable, it will never become dangerous, becaufe the veneration of the people towards their paftors will be granted them but in proportion as their conduêt is conformable to the rules of that morality they teach; and religion in every nation enjoins them integrity, and no lefs ftriêtly prohibits them from intriguing.　Is it by degrading that religion, that they are to be infpired with the defire of doing it honor by their lives?

But what need, fay you, of myfteries, what occafion for dogmas?　Why this belief required to abfurdities which are contrary to reafon, and which we cannot even pretend to admit without blufhing to have been capable of acknowledging them?　&c.

I always

I always leave to divines, to teachers who are honored with this miniftry, the care of juftifying the revelation, of eftablifhing its truths; but I afk you, in the name of that reafon whofe rights you think you are defending, what you find humiliating in its myfteries? They are incomprehenfible, as has been already obferved by writers more eloquent than myfelf: but does it neceffarily follow that they are abfurd? Is not every thing in nature myfterious to you; and is every thing therefore impoffible or extravagant?

For inftance, is not fight a myftery? Can you affign any reafon, why that ray of light which is invifible when it is not reflected, acquires, when thrown on any object, the faculty of ftriking your eye, and of irritating your nerves? Can you conceive how it is not itfelf which is fenfible of it, but the furface whence it is reflected, and whereof it has received the impreffion?

This common miracle, this daily myftery, you notwithftanding give credit to; you avail yourfelf of it; you conceive it no degradation to enjoy the pleafure of a beautiful landfcape or a grand view, although the mode in which the immenfity of the objects which are made to pafs over the optic nerves, is to you wholly incomprehenfible:

prehenfible—why then are you more captious on the myfteries of religion?

But faith does not depend on you! Be it fo. Silence, however, is within your power—once again, what compels you to break it? A man born blind would not be required to believe in the prodigies of light; he is deficient in the organ neceffary to enable him to form an idea of it. Did he content himfelf with a filent denial of the fact, others would reft fatisfied with lamenting his infatuation; did he even declare aloud in his own chamber, that thefe are abfurdities, and that it indicates imbecility to admit them; were he, in fupport of his fyftem, to multiply pleafantries, and even witticifms, which he might do with little effort—indulgence would ftill accompany our pity.

But were he to cry aloud in the ftreet, that it argues a man to be a fool to have windows in his houfe, and that the architects who conftruct them are knaves; if he threw ftones at, and began to break them with his ftick; if at the alarm thus given, other blind men, and even fuch as faw clearly, but were ill difpofed, affembled together, and all announced the difpofition together with the fymptoms of a tumult, would it not be neceffary to run?

Would

Would it not be allowable to ufe féverity towards fuch a demagogue and his profelytes?

Did the religious ceremonies of the prefent day carry with them, like thofe of old, that fanguinary and fhocking appearance which filled the temples; were your organs lacerated by the howlings of victims, affailed by the ftench of the fat of burnt flefh or of blood, your averfion might be excufable, although you could not juftify it by the example of thofe great men to whom you refer as your predeceffors and models in revolting againft the religious fyftems of their times.

The philofophic Julian not only did not difpife or fly from thefe facrifices, but he affifted at and was perfonally engaged in them; he was himfelf the high prieft, and himfelf afforded an example to thofe butchering pontiffs, of whom he was ambitious to be the head. Scipio, when fummoned and accufed before the Roman people, difdained making a defence, but difdained not to go to give thanks to the gods for thofe victories, which, in his opinion, feemed fufficient for his apology: he haughtily retired from the tribunal to which he was cited, but it was to proftrate himfelf at the foot of the altars, and to load them with victims. Socrates, when dying a martyr to deifm, ordered a

cock

cock to be facrificed to Efculapius. His laft words were an homage to the gods and to the religion of his country.

Thus, were you born under a fyftem which phyfically required the blood of animals, in order to poffefs the privilege of excufing your internal incredulity by the example of thefe celebrated men, it would be likewife neceffary to imitate them in their external conformity to eftablifhed rites and ceremonies: but Chriftianity has purged its altars from this afflictive barbarity. It has fubftituted, in lieu of thefe maffacres, a peaceful offering, which is neither offenfive to the fight or the underftanding; even phyfically confidered it is an emblem of peace and union: regarding it in a political point of view, the fentiments it excites, are concord, a love of mankind, and gratitude towards the Almighty. Were this fyftem diftinguifhed by no other advantage, it would be fufficient to merit the regard of a benevolent philofopher; and the real power, the profundity of its principles, the impracticability of tearing them up without endangering the civil conftitutions with which they are now incorporated, are fo many decifive confiderations which fhould, in a modern Confucius of really benevolent fentiments, extinguifh the wifh to deftroy it, were it even poffible.

And

And how many additional motives, even admitting this poſſibility, would concur in impoſing ſilence on every true philoſopher, on men more emulous of confirming the peace and union of ſociety, than ambitious of the ſad honor of eſtabliſhing a reputation by breaking through thoſe ties which extend to, and encircle its various claſſes?

I ſhall not examine whether this boaſted Deiſm of the preſent day, be not in effect an Atheiſm, veiled under the ſlender qualification of the term: if this Divinity, without prieſts and miniſters, ſequeſtered in the ideal heaven wherein he is concealed, is a more efficient Being than the ſenſeleſs and inactive Deity of Epicurus.

I ſhall not enquire whether this voluntary, ſpiritual, and ſecret communion, this internal worſhip tacitly offered up to a Deity without any ſenſible influence, and ſolely pointed out by reaſon, is as firm and efficacious a check to thoſe deſires and paſſions which are contrary to the general order of ſociety, as that of a religion ſupported by the dignity of its ceremonies, the purity of its moral precepts, the majeſty of its dogmas, and by the pomp even with which its miniſters are ſurrounded. I am willing to ſuppoſe it.

I am even willing to admit, that its aſcendancy will be the ſame over all men, upon

S every

every mind, and over all ranks of fociety : I
will fuppofe, that the cool difcuffions of the philofopher founded on principles of reafon, and
demonftrating wide of the occafion, the advantage or difadvantage to arife, whether from refiftance or compliance, will have equal influence
on the mind with the power of the infpired Pontiff, holding out rewards and punifhments from
God himfelf, who continually repeating threats
and promifes, to be realized hereafter, exercifes
a jurifdiction, fevere and formidable even at
prefent, from its clofe affinity with a future ftate
of retribution. All this I fuppofe: and doubtlefs it is doing no injuftice to philofophy, to
grant its power and effects to be equal to thofe
of religion.——

Even in this cafe, between two different modes
of maintaining good order which fhall poffefs
equal efficacy, is not the preference due to that
already eftablifhed ? I am in poffeffion of a building, which affures me a fufficient fhelter to my
wants; are you excufable in throwing it down,
merely becaufe you can fubftitute another which
will poffefs the like advantages ?

Deifm is founded, fay you, on good order, a
love of virtue, and fentiments of brotherly love
among mankind: which I grant. But has religion any other object ? Its minifters have

4   paffions

paffions and frailties!—but will your philofophers be exempt from them?

The formalities of religion are irkfome; the duties it enjoins are fatiguing; it requires a fub-miffion grievous to be borne; its priefts exact not only a belief in their doctrines, but refpect to themfelves. This is true—but regarding it with you, merely as a civil eftablifhment, a po-litical inftitution formed to confolidate the edi-fice of fociety, to enfure the general repofe of all thofe who are affembled together to enjoy the benefits of mutual intercourfe; is not this form, this duty, this fubmiffion, and this refpect, in-difpenfably neceffary?

Would you deny a fovereign the right of having his guards, a magiftrate his lictors, beadles, door-keepers? &c. Do you confider as an ufurpation on their part, the fubmiffion which is fhewn them, and the veneration they require? Why then fuch acrimony were it even more unjuft and humiliating, at the deference fhewn to a mitre or a ftole, which you approve when addreffed to a diadem or a blue, yellow, or red ribbon?

Nothing certainly can be lefs philofophic and more childifh than this diftinction; it would not even be deemed pardonable in the populace, among the ignorant and vulgar, who are guided

by

by appearances alone, and who finding fomething
more ftriking in military evolutions, than in ec-
clefiaftical ceremonies, confent with lefs reluct-
ance to bend the knee to the haughty comman-
der of the former, than the peaceful director of
the latter.   But is it poffible that enlightened
men, who boaft themfelves fuperior to prejudice,
and who form their judgment of things by
their intrinfic worth; can thus become dupes to
their fenfes, and think it a degradation to proftrate themfelves before one uniform, more than
another ?

You feel indignant at the deference you are
conftrained to fhew to a rector or a bifhop; but
foon after you will find that irkfome which is
due to a fheriff, an alderman, a bailiff, a chan-
cellor, or a king: all thefe gradations of obedience have an affinity with, and tend mutually
to the fupport of each other.   Your philofophy
would be inconfiftent, if after having broken
one of thefe links, it were to be more fcrupu-
loufly bound by the other.—Viewing them both
as mere human inftitutions, once again, they
muft poffefs the fame force or the fame impo-
tence : it is the moft terrible diforder then in fact,
which your opinions have a tendency to introduce—even without your wifhing it—you are the

declared

declared enemy of fociety at large, whilft pro-
feffing yourfelf that of its tyrants only.

And what would be the refult, were I to trace
in the lower ranks the baleful effects of this fyftem of independence, which you affert in the
name of humanity, and to maintain, as you fay,
the dignity of our fpecies? I continue to queftion
in your reformation none of thofe benefits which
you attribute to it: I am willing to fuppofe that
Deifm, once admitted and univerfally believed,
will conduce equally to the public good with
any other fyftem; that a philofopher, from his
clofet, will warm the minds of men equally by
a good moral effay, as a preacher or rector by
his public difcourfes or private and verbal exhortations; that a finner, or a man who is
tempted to become fo, will be recalled to his
duty as forcibly by the view of a Lyceum as
of a Church; that academies of virtue, like
thofe of language and phyfical inveftigation,
will be eftablifhed, and that thefe fine geniufes,
whilft elegantly debating on morality, will operate as fuccefsfully towards its fupport, as a numerous and regular clergy now do, whofe principal and even fole duty it is to fulfil this
office.

But a certain time muft neceffarily elapfe between the ancient fervitude of mens minds and

their

their new independence. The only way of arriving at that fublime and purified point your
philofophy aims at, muft be by bringing thefe
rites and habits of flavery into contempt. This
interval may perhaps be fafely paffed over by fome
minds more refined, better organized, or fecured
from the dangers of temptation by a competent
fortune, or a want of opportunity to do ill.

Thefe will not confider their duty as done
away, with thofe acceffary aids which had formerly accompanied the theory. Be it fo. But
the great body of mankind, whom you think it
effential to enlighten, and whom it is certainly
of very great importance to reftrain; that body
of men who in every thing lie open to temptation, becaufe throughout life they are on every
fide bounded by neceffity; that people to whom
every minute brings with it fome want, and
every ftep reminds them of fome conftraint; will
the like reflections and an equal 'difcretion attend them? When all men are become Philofophers and Deifts, it will no longer be neceffary
for them to be Chriftians. I grant it: but in the
time of their education, in the interval fet apart
to free them from their old prejudices, and infpire them with new lights, how will they act?

Will they be capable of feparating the virtue
they are to love and to practife, from that principle

ciple which inftilled it? a principle which you teach them to fly from and deteft. Will they be capable of confining to external forms merely, that contempt which you recommend towards the late objects of their adoration, and confider themfelves ftill bound by duty, when they are no longer fo, by thofe vifible habits, intended to enforce its obfervance?

If you hefitate for a reply, every enlightened man, even among your own partizans, many of thofe whom you have amufed and perverted, will they not make it for you? See what paffes in that fociety wherein you enjoy a triumph apparently fo flattering, where you have in reality formed a feminary, not of difciples, but preachers, as bold and as zealous as yourfelf—

Every thing is there appreciated, every thing difcuffed, and every thing fubverted; but what is the confequence? Afk the magiftrate invefted with the fevere duty of punifhing crimes, and you will hear if he does not mourn to fee the number of them increafe, in proportion as the influence of that peaceful miniftry is weakened, which was deftined to their prevention.

As to thofe crimes which the law cannot ftrike at, becaufe they are either too fecret in their nature, or of a defcription for which there are no

punifh-

punifhments provided; with regard to thofe
which introduce diforder into families, by deftroying thofe principles on which their felicity
depends; confult the general voice of mankind
to know whether Deifm or Religion is beft calculated to reprefs them. Will you dare to affert, that it is in philofophic families we are to
look for models of filial refpect, conjugal love,
fincerity in friendfhip, or fidelity among do-
meftics? And were you difpofed to do fo, would
not your own confcience, your own experience,
fupprefs this falfhood even before your lips could
utter it?

And were thefe melancholy effects of a licentioufnefs, decorated indeed with too many great
names, confined to the circle of thofe families
wherein it difcovers itfelf with moft impunity, the
real philofopher and friend to mankind might
reft content with a filent figh; but its influence
extends to every rank of fociety, and to men of
all underftandings. The footman, who, while
waiting at table, fees men entitled to the rank
of gentlemen, affembled together to turn that
prelate into ridicule who teaches him to be
faithful, and inculcates that doctrine which alone
affures him of the reward attending it; would
be weak indeed, if he did not foon think it ridiculous to perfift in his integrity.

If

If a happy frame of mind, or the fear of the gallows, prevent him from realizing in his conduct the confequence of this more than indifcreet converfation, he will be the echo and propagator of it: as a man in health who has touched one infected with the plague, may communicate the infection without being difeafed himfelf.

This epidemic evil notwithftanding, fpreads itfelf abroad; it reaches to the workman fecluded in his garret, and to the peafant dying with hunger and defpair in his cottage; they are alike taught to compare their wants and miferies with the value of thofe fcruples which prolong them; they no longer go to hear the minifter who holds out to them in his fermon the hope of being one day compenfated; who at confeffion counteracts the progrefs of temptation in order to withdraw them from it. And what is the confequence of this terrible emancipation? Muft it not either lead to crime or defpair under every preffure of neceffity? and does not the one almoft neceffarily produce the other?

It is here more efpecially that we perceive the prodigious difference between the arbitrary fpeculations of philofophy, and the real utility of religion; which uniting a fublime theory with cuftomary duties, at the fame time repreffes and confoles.

foles. The former indeed, reccommends the practice of truth, moderation, obedience to the laws, and a regard to the property of others: this is the language of reafon, or rather of intereft; policy alone is fufficient to inform us, that, in order to exercife our own rights, we muft refpect thofe of others: but in all this I perceive only fecurities raifed in favor of opulence. What return does philofophy offer to the wretch for thofe fetters fhe lays upon him, when the poffeffions of the rich are at hand?

Does fhe enter his cottage through the filth that furrounds and infects it? Does fhe place herfelf befide that bed of forrows, of the horrors of which, the devouring malady which confumes him is oftentimes the leaft? Does fhe offer in the compaffionate vifitor who exhorts him, the reprefentative of a juft God, about to indemnify him in another life for his fufferings in this? Does fhe enjoin on this eloquent differtator the duty of feconding the future hope he holds out in his words, with an effectual prefent relief?

The philofopher who fhould fometimes fulfil this duty of benevolence, would be confidered as a prodigy of virtue. Religion impofes it on its minifters as the commoneft of all their duties, and a daily function which they cannot hold themfelves excufed from without being guilty of a crime,

nor

nor defer without betraying their holy office. They, in common with the philofopher, are protectors of the poffeffions of the rich; but, beyond him, they confole the poor under the privation of them. The latter, in every fenfe degraded, reduced at every inftant to envy the lot of the animals of whom it is his greateft happinefs to be the companion, and oftentimes flave; exercifes even in his mifery, a fort of empire over his paftor: he feems no otherwife related to fociety than through thofe remonftrances which juftify the hardfhip by which he is facrificed to its general good. It is only when exhorted, to fee himfelf tamely deprived of every right of humanity, that he is allowed to fufpect himfelf a man.

Were even religion juftly chargeable with all thofe evils with which you falfely accufe it; were it true that in fome unhappy times, and at certain confined intervals, fhe had introduced diforder into fome periods in hiftory; would not the fervices fhe unceafingly renders to every clafs of fociety, and which it is even her very effence to beftow, have long fince more than expiated them?

Let us then ceafe to decry and to attack it— were it true that we might flatter ourfelves with being able to effect its overthrow, it would be a

real

real crime to attempt it. If its interpreters and minifters fometimes lofe fight of the object of their duty and vocation, the philofopher may take upon him to recal them to it; but not by proclaiming an infurrection againft them, or by endeavours to render them odious and ridiculous: whatever are his private opinions, I think he fhould ufe his talents and his fuperiority of genius, to imprefs their feveral obligations and duties on every order of the ftate, and not to degrade, difcourage, or deftroy any one.

Addreffing himfelf to the *clergy*, he ought to fay, " Be virtuous and indulgent, that you may " be revered and ufeful: to the *people*, refpect " the laws, which enfure your property; the " civil power, which protects them; and the " religious one, which defends the firft from the " invafions of the latter: and to *kings*, love and " maintain religion; fhew an example of the " practice of it in your own conduct, becaufe " even to yourfelf it is a fafer fecurity than " a thoufand regiments; revere its minifters, " whofe afcendancy over the people depends in " a degree on the countenance you fhew them; " reftrain them if they wander, and they will " never deviate from their duty if your favor is " the fruit of a faithful performance of it; fuffer " not the principles of your faith to be difcuffed, " they

" they are fixed; permit them, not to be defended
" any more than attacked. Never perfecute
" thofe who having the misfortune not to believe
" in them, at leaft are prudent enough to fup-
" prefs their incredulity; but punifh with feverity
" fuch as fhall dare to difplay it with licentiouf-
" nefs; reprefs them, not fo much to vindicate
" the glory of God which thefe crimes cannot
" affect, as to preferve the civil order of fociety,
" which they have a tendency to difturb."

In holding fuch a language, a philofopher
worthy of the name, would become the mediator
between every eftablifhment; he would be the
univerfal benefactor of mankind.

It is to be regretted that Mr. Voltaire did not
attend to this truth, or that too ardent an imagination prevented him from being fenfible of its
importance. A mind like his would have embellifhed, and given it additional force. Here
it poffeffes but the plain and unadorned language
of reafon. I would afk pardon of his fhade, at
the foot of his tomb, for the freedom of this remark, if the juftice I have done him in other
refpects, and a regard for the public good, did
not authorife its feverity.

www.ingramcontent.com/pod-product-compliance
Lightning Source LLC
Chambersburg PA
CBHW020344030726
47496CB00007B/1998